THE U.S. ARMY AT

CAMP BEWDLEY

AND LOCATIONS IN THE WYRE FOREST AREA

1943 - 1945

Adrian and Neil Turley

First edition

Published February 2000
by
Adrian & Neil Turley
1 Orchard Rise
Bewdley
Worcestershire DY12 2EW

© A & N Turley 2000

All rights reserved. No part of this book may be reproduced
or transmitted in any form or by any means, electronic
or mechanical without permission of the publishers.

ISBN 0-9537869-0-0

Printed by :   A. J. Domone & Sons
7 - 9 Rowland Way
Hoo Farm Ind Est
Kidderminster
Worcestershire DY11 7RA

THE U.S ARMY AT

CAMP BEWDLEY

AND LOCATIONS IN THE WYRE FOREST AREA

1943 – 1945

Acknowledgements

National Archives, Washington

U.S Army Military History Institute, Carlisle Barracks

Patton Museum of Cavalry and Armor, Fort Knox

Dwight D. Eisenhower Library

Bolling Air Force Base

National Monuments Record (English Heritage)

Public Records Office, Kew

Worcester Evening News

Kidderminster Shuttle

Maj. Gen.(Ret) Hugh F Foster Jr U.S.A

Lt. Col.(Ret) Hugh F Foster III U.S.A

Alfred W Farris Jr	*Stanley Watkins*
Lillian R Swerdlow	*Don Wilcox*
Kenneth G Wakefield	*Brian Knight*
Phil Aldridge	*John P Thomson*
Steve Braginton	*John Harper*
Doris Hoskins	*Gertrude Westwood*

CONTENTS

Introduction .... Page 6

VIII Corps 8

XII Corps 15

       93rd Signal Battalion 25
       3rd Auxilliary Surgical Group 26
       Tank Destroyer and Armored Groups 27
       2nd Cavalry Group 28
       QM Truck Companies 30
       Liaison Aircraft, Weather and
       Communication Squadrons 31

The Hospitals 33

       The American Red Cross 36
       297th General Hospital 38
       Reminiscences of a 297 G.H Nurse 52
       114th General Hospital 60
       Hospital Train Unloading Procedures 65
       52nd General Hospital 69
       Field Hospitals 75

Dog Lane Camp, Bewdley 68

Salute the Soldier Week, Kidderminster 77

U.S.A.A.F Station 509 80

90th Infantry Division 82

Tented Camps 85

Supply Depot DP2-G24 86

Hospital Trains 87

Introduction

Bolero ...... The codeword for the build up of U.S troops and supplies in the United Kingdom in preparation for the cross-channel invasion.

Included in the Bolero plan were six convertible installations known as dual purpose camps designed to serve as general hospitals after D-Day, but so planned that the ward buildings could be used as barracks for combat troops until that time.

Two of these dual purpose camps were to be situated on 102 1/2 acres of land at Burlish, bounded on one side by the Bewdley to Stourport railway and extending towards the Kidderminster Borough boundary at Birchen Coppice.

The land, owned by Kidderminster Corporation although outside the Borough boundary, was requisitioned by the War Office on 18 September 1942 under the Defence Regulations of 1938.

Construction of the camps was completed by late summer 1943, advance detachments of U.S Army troops arriving during November 1943.

The installations were known by the U.S Army as Camp Bewdley, the lower camp near Burlish Crossing designated Camp No.1, the upper camp at Burlish Top designated Camp No.2.

By the end of May 1944 the number of U.S troops in the United Kingdom had reached 1,526,965, of which over 4,000 were at Camp Bewdley and a further 10,000 in tented camps within a few miles to the north of Bewdley.

Prior to D-Day the upper camp was an important administrative Command Post, being the Headquarters of the VIII Corps and subsequently the XII Corps. These units were charged with the reception, supervision and training of First Army Group Reserve and Third Army units arriving in the United Kingdom.

After D-Day both camps were to become the home of two General Hospital units, receiving 12,000 battle casualties from Europe.

In July 1942 work commenced on building a large hospital installation at Wolverley. January 1943 saw the arrival of the 52nd General Hospital Unit which was to remain at Wolverley until June 1945, providing medical care for the sick and wounded. The hospital handled over 20,000 such patients during its period of operation.

Although this book covers the principal U.S Army units stationed in the Bewdley area during WW2 there were numerous other small units either stationed or staging in the district.

Where extracts have been taken from unit histories the American spelling of certain words has been retained.

DIAGRAMMATIC SKETCH SHOWING LOCATION OF BEWDLEY AND KIDDERMINSTER CAMPS

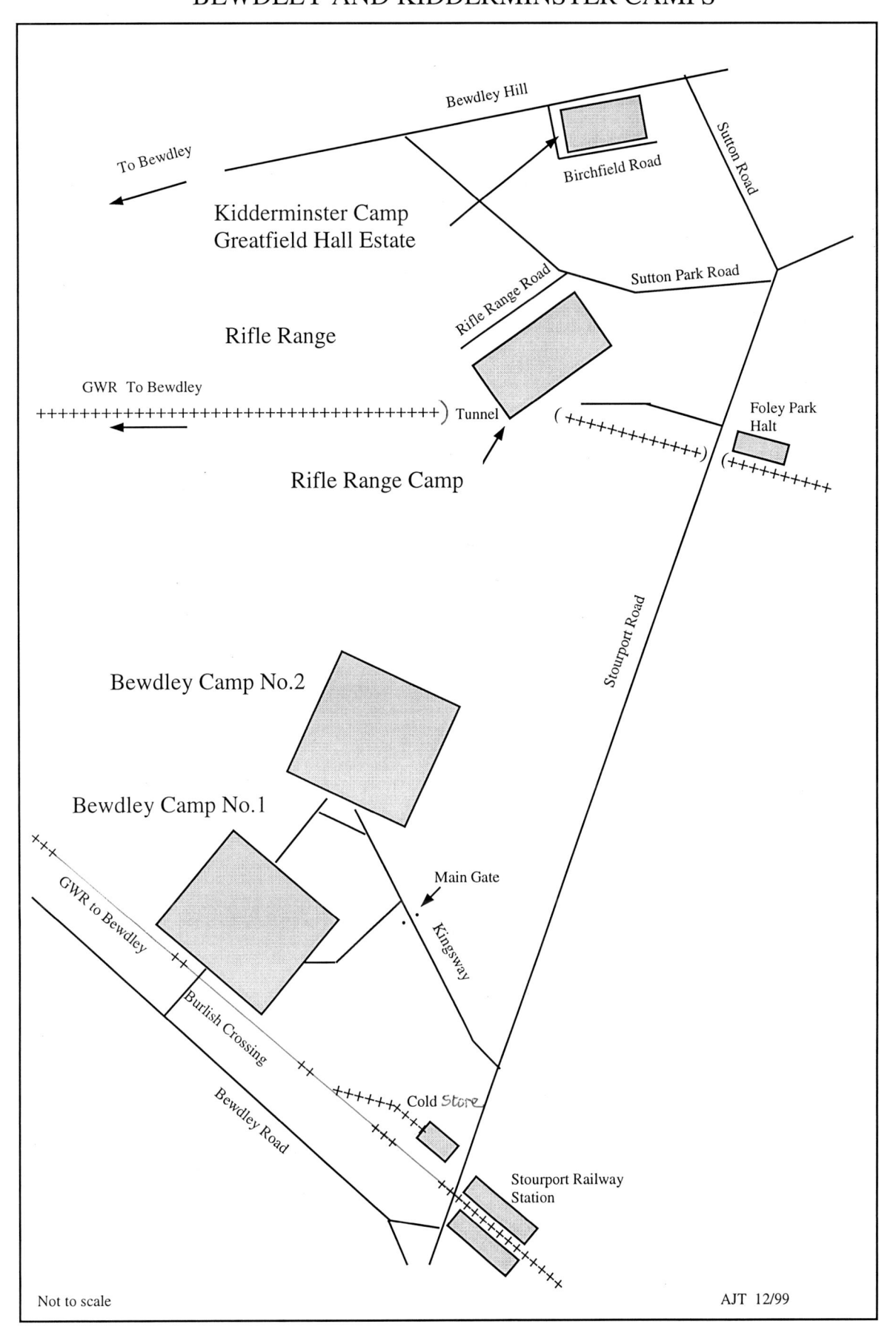

VIII CORPS

Commanding General : Major General Emil F Reinhardt.

The VIII Headquarters was alerted for overseas movement in October 1943, while on maneuvers in Louisiana. Movement orders for an advance detachment were received and this group entrained on 16 November 1943. The movement orders for the main body and the VIII Headquarters departed from its home station at Brownwood, Texas on 28 November 1943 and detrained at Fort Slocum, New York on 30 November 1943.

After a short period of preparation at Fort Slocum the Headquarters embarked on the transport ship "Aquitania" on 11 December 1943, sailing on the following day. They disembarked at Greenock, Scotland on 20 December 1943 and were transported by train to Camp Bewdley, Worcestershire, England, the assigned station.

Upon arrival at Camp Bewdley the VIII Corps began a period of indoctrination and preparation for the mission outlined by the European Theater Commander.

The mission was as follows:

"The Commanding General, VIII Corps is charged with the administration, supply and supervision of training of troops comprising the First Army Group Reserve, and will communicate directly with this Headquarters on these matters except as otherwise directed in specific instances."

[By command of Lieutenant General Devers in letter from Headquarters, European Theater of Operations, U.S Army dated 23 December 1943.]

Corps Organisation

Headquarters

Section	Officers	Enlisted Men
Commanding General	3	1
Chief of Staff	8	1
Asst. Chief of Staff G1	3	4
Asst. Chief of Staff G2	6	6
Asst. Chief of Staff G3	6	8
Asst. Chief of Staff G4	5	5
Engineer	4	8
Signal	4	6
Chemical	2	3
Medical	5	4
Ordnance	6	12
Adjutant General	5	23
Inspector General	4	3
Judge Advocate	2	3
Quartermaster	4	5
Chaplain	3	3
Finance	2	6
Special Service	2	5
Red Cross	1	0
C.I.C Detachment	0	13
TOTAL	**75**	**119**

Headquarters Company

	Officers	Enlisted Men
Company Hq	2	17
Supply	1	22
Mess	1	23
Transportation	1	31
TOTAL	**5**	**93**

	Officers	Enlisted Men
Medical Detachment	2	8
TOTAL	**2**	**8**

Section	Officers	Enlisted Men
Military Police Platoon		
Headquarters	2	8
1st Squadron	0	9
2nd Squadron	0	9
3rd Squadron	0	9
4th Squadron	0	9
TOTAL	2	44
HQ and HQ Artillery Battery		
Headquarters	6	0
S2	5	0
S3	5	0
S4	2	0
Battery Hq	2	14
Operations	2	26
TOTAL	22	40
Communications Platoon		
Headquarters	1	4
Wire	0	24
Radio	0	8
Maintenance	0	17
TOTAL	1	53

Total Strength ------------- 107 Officers
357 Enlisted Men

On 13 March 1944 the VIII Corps was assigned to the Third United States Army. The Commanding General, Major General Emil F Reinhardt was replaced by Major General Troy H Middleton.

Major General Reinhardt returned to the United States to command the 69th Infantry Division, U.S First Army. He was to have the honour of being present at the historic official meeting between the Allied military leaders following the link up between First Army and Russian patrols at the River Elbe, Torgau, Germany on 26 April 1945.

Major General Emil F Reinhardt signed his name in the visitors book during his visit to Bewdley Guildhall to meet local dignitaries on 20 December 1943.

Major General Emil F.Reinhardt, Commanding General of VIII Corps was at Camp Bewdley from December 1943 until March 1944.
Photo : U.S Arrmy

Photo : U.S Signal Corps

Major General Emil F. Reinhardt greets Major General Vladimir Rusakov, commander of the Russian 59th Infantry Division, after epoch making link up of American and Russian units at the Elbe River, east of Tolgau, Germany. 26 April 1945.

Extracts from VIII Corps Activity Reports dated 7 April 1944

G-3 Section [Operation and Training]

From the arrival of the Corps Headquarters at Camp Bewdley until 10 January 1944, the G-3 Section was occupied in orientation, physical organisation and preparing plans for supervising the training of troops to be assigned to this headquarters. During this time, local defense and alert plans for the camp site were developed.

On 10 January 1944, the Corps was given its first troop assignment in the United Kingdom. The G-3 Section was immediately faced with the problem of supervising and training of a large number of small organisations whose particular training problems were almost individual. This, of course, was due to the fact that most of these units were Army Reserve troops, and in general, were small units requiring high standards in technical training to undertake specialized missions. In an effort to quickly orientate the new units as they arrived from the United States, the G-3 Section prepared a training directive. This directive was, of necessity, very broad in scope in order to fit the multitudiness of problems of our assigned troops. This orientation process was furthered by talks to officers of newly reported units by officers of this section, the full time efforts of two officers has been required to handle the matter of training areas, ranges and schools.

Each unit assigned or attached to the Corps has been visited within 5 days after its arrival, a preliminary inspection made and the unit commander thoroughly orientated and assisted in every way. Thereafter at least one visit per month has been made. As a result of these visits, accurate and up-to-date information as to the status of the unit has always been available and in addition, valuable assistance has been rendered each unit in expediting the unit's equipment and in other ways.

These problems can be understood when considering that 314 distinct organisations have been handled by this Corps ranging in size from separate detachments of a postal unit through airborne and armored divisions.

G-4 Section [Supply]

In addition to the normal duties connected with the operation of a G-4 Section of a separate Corps, this section was charged with the supervision of receiving units arriving in the United Kingdom. After arrival of this Headquarters and prior to 13 March 1944, this section briefed reception parties and assisted in securing additional transportation and supplies for 110 units ranging in size from companies to divisions. On 13 March 1944 this Headquarters was assigned to the Third United States Army, but continued with the duties of reception of units for both the Third United States Army and VIII Corps.

Signal Section

Upon arrival at Camp Bewdley the Corps Signal Section was active in the installation of communication facilities for the Corps Headquarters. The advance party of the Signal Section had already set up and had in operation a temporary telephone installation when the Corps arrive. A detachment from the 50th Signal Battalion furnished the personnel for the operation of the switchboard and message center. About the 10 January 1944 the switchboard operation was taken over by the newly arrived 59th Signal Battalion.

The permanent switchboard setup, a six multiple board was installed and ready for operation by 24 February 1944, This service utilized forty trunk lines and furnished service for 200 subscribers, approximately 375 extensions.

The Signal Section was successful in obtaining 17 private wires as follows:

    3 to ETOUSA [London]
    2 to 1st Army H.Q. [Bristol]
    3 to 3rd Army H.Q. [Knutsford, Cheshire]
    2 to Services of Supply [Cheltenham]
    2 to Eastern Base Section [Watford]
    2 to Southern Base Section [Wilton, Salisbury]
    2 to Western Base Section [Chester]
    2 to Northern Ireland Base Section [Belfast]

The VIII Corps Message Center established courier services and connections with GHQ messenger service that made the volume of business second only to that handled by ETOUSA's Message Center.

Units at Camp Bewdley ..... 1 March 1944

    VIII Corps Hq & Hq Co (w/attchd Med)
    VIII Corps Artillery. Hq & Hq Battery
    MP Platoon VIII Corps
    13th Machine Records Unit
    59th Signal Battalion
    246th Signal Company (Opns)
    4th Signal Center Team
    6th Signal Center Team
    665th Topographic Corps (Engineers)
    3516th Medium Auto Maintenance Company
    3rd Auxilliary Surgical Group
    8th Armored Group
    1st Tank Destroyer Brigade. Hq & Hq Company

The VIII Corps changed permanent stations from Camp Bewdley, Worcestershire to Marbury Park, Cheshire on 12 April 1944 by authority of Operational Movement Order No.58, Headquarters VIII Corps, dated 8 April 1944. The administration of Camp Bewdley being left in the lap of the advance detachment of the XII Corps until the arrival of the main body.

Under Third Army, the following mission was received:

"Responsibility for receiving all army units assigned or attached to Third United States Army is fixed upon Headquarters VIII Corps. Accommodations and Assignment Sections ETOUSA and VIII Corps are permitted to contact each other directly on this subject."

(Paraphrase from Headquarters Third Army to Commanding General VIII Corps.)

Photo : National Archives

Major General Troy H.Middleton
Commanding General VIII Corps
at Camp Bewdley from March 1944

The first week of May 1944, during a conference at Supreme Headquarters in London, General Bradley of the First Army expressed his desire to have an additional Corps to participate in the invasion as a reserve. This request was granted and VIII Corps was assigned to this mission. As a result of this assignment and mission, VIII Corps was the fourth Corps to land on the continent, preceded by the V Corps, VII Corps and XIX Corps.

The VIII Corps moved from England to the Continent in three echelons.

1. The advance detail, composed of 27 Officers and 2 Warrant Officers, departed from Marbury Park and arrived at Blandford on 1 June 1944, then proceeded to Southampton on 11 June and boarded ship the following day.

2. The second echelon departed from Marbury Park on 16 June 1944 for Dorchester. They departed from Dorchester on 23 June 1944 and sailed from Southampton the following day, arriving at Utah Beach on 26 June.

3. The third echelon departed from Marbury Park on 21 June 1944 for Reservoir Camp, Gloucester. They left Reservoir Camp and arrived at Marshalling Area B-5 on 30 June. Departed Marshalling Area for Southampton on 2 July 1944 and boarded the SS "Belva Lockwood" arriving at Utah Beach the following day.

XII CORPS

Commanding General : Major General Gilbert R Cook.

The advance party of XII Corps boarded the "Duchess of Bedford", a Canadian Pacific liner, and departed from the New York Port of Embarkation on 23 March 1944. The voyage took eleven days, the liner anchoring on the Clyde on 3 April 1944.

The party entrained at 1100 hours and travelled to Crewe; thence by truck to Marbury Hall, near Northwich, Cheshire. Late on 4 April they moved again and on the following day were at the site of the XII Corps first Command Post in England ..... Camp Bewdley, Worcestershire, preparing to receive the rest of the headquarters when it should arrive.

The main body of the headquarters travelled on the "Queen Mary", or SS490 as she was known, departing from New York on 10 April 1944. At about 2100 hours on the 16 April the XII Corps reached the River Clyde. The green pleasant hills, the light coloured cottages with red roofs of the ancient kingdom of Scotland looked friendly, and very near at hand. The Firth of Clyde was full of vessels, including many naval craft, among which were observed several "flat tops".

Disembarkation was by harbour tug the following day. A kilted Scots band featuring squealing bagpipes, and positively said to be from a famous regiment, assisted the headquarters entrainment which was accomplished right on the pier. The neat, foreign looking British railway cars occasioned much comment. The engine in particular was judged hardly big enough to pull a toy train, but as it started southward from Scotland to England it could be noted that it was picking up a very creditable speed. At the first stop, flocks of children clustered about the train, chanting a chorus that would become monotonously familiar to members of the XII Corps before they quit the U.K ...."Any gum chum?"

At 0630 on 18 April 1944, in the early morning light and a whisp of fog, which later proved to be unusual thereabouts, the goodly company rolled into Stourport, in Worcestershire, close to the River Severn.

Camp Bewdley was described as "a pretty little camp, a well drained camp, not muddy. At the foot of the hill was Stourport and also at the foot of the hill was a small arms range from which at least once bullets came whining up into the camp. Along the ridge, a short distance away to the north east, stood the sizable town of Kidderminster, soon to be dear to the hearts of many XII Corps men. Not far to the west, over beyond the little hamlet of Bewdley, that gave its name to the camp, could be seen the rolling wooded highlands of the Wyre Forest, and all about lay the farms and tiny picturesque settlements of rural England."

Units at Camp Bewdley .... 5 May 1944
Per XII Corps Station List No.1 dated 5 May 1944

    Headquarters XII Corps (Building 122)
    Headquarters Company XII Corps (with attached medical)
    Military Police Platoon XII Corps
    Headquarters XII Corps Artillery
    Headquarters Battery XII Corps Artillery
    Company "C" 511 Military Police Battalion
    93rd Signal Battalion
    301st Signal Operations Battalion (Detachment)
    3345 QM Truck Company
    94th Medical Gas Treatment Battalion (Advance Detachment)

    2nd Cavalry Group Hq and Hq Troop
    2nd Cavalry Squadron
    42nd Cavalry Squadron
    3rd Auxiliary Surgical Group
    8th Armored Group Hq and Hq Company

On 26 April 1944, key staff officers of XII Corps went up to the Third Army War Room in Peover Hall, near Knutsford in Cheshire, for a briefing. The selected members of the Corps learned that day of Operation "Bolero", the code name for the building up of men and materials in the U.K for the assault of Fortress Europe. Covered in greater detail was the plan to become famous as "Overlord", the operation to carry "Bolero" into France.

General Patton's visit to Camp Bewdley

The following is an extract from the XII Corps history - "XII Corps - Spearhead of Patton's Third Army" by Lt. Col. George Dyer (1947).

... General Patton arrived at Camp Bewdley on 31 May 1944 to deliver a characteristic talk to the officers and men of the XII Corps. By the accident that there was among the men who could and did, take down the speech word for word in shorthand, and who later circulated the copies of the transcription, this talk has since become celebrated as the type the general was supposed always to give to troops. The member of the XII Corps headquarters who preserved this classic also left an original description of events at Camp Bewdley leading up to the speech itself. It is given below, almost intact, because it presents a fresh point of view on the life of the corps headquarters and units in England, because it provides a parting glimpse of the first XII Corps commander, Lt Gen Simpson, and because it is a minor masterpiece of its kind. The writer, for reasons which no doubt seem good to him, has chosen to remain anonymous:

"The big camp buzzed with tension. For the hundreds of eager ETO rookies, newly arrived from the States , it was a great day in their lives. This day marked their first taste of 'the real thing'. For now they were not puppets in brown going through the motions of soldiering, with 3,000 miles of water between them and English soil, but actually in the heart of Britain itself, awaiting the coming of that legendary figure, Lt Gen George S Patton, 'Old Blood and Guts' himself, about whom many a colorful chapter will be written for the schoolboys of tomorrow. Patton, of the brisk, purposeful stride, the harsh compelling voice, the lurid vocabulary, the grim indomitable spirit that carried him through glory with his army in Africa and Sicily. 'America's fightingest general' they called him. He was not a 'Desk Commando', but the man who was sent for when the going got rough and a fighter was needed. The most hated and feared American of all on the part of the German Army. Patton was coming, and the stage was being set. He would address the XII Corps of his own Third Army, of which he had only lately been put in command - a move that might have a far-reaching effect on the global war that at the moment was a secret in the files at Washington.

"The new men saw the camp turn out en masse for the first time in full uniform. Today their marching was not lackadaisical. It was serious, and the men felt the difference, from the lieutenants in charge of the companies on down. In long columns they marched down the hill from the barracks, counting cadence, turned left up the rise and so down to the roped off field where the general was to speak. Gold braid and stripes were everywhere. Soon, company by company, the hillside was a solid mass of brown. It was a beautiful spring morning, the tall trees lining the road swaying gently in the breeze. Across the field a British farmer was calmly tilling his soil. High upon a hill a group of English huddled together awaiting the coming of the general. MPs in white leggings, belts and helmets were everywhere, brisk and grim. Twitterings of birds could be heard above the dull murmur of the crowd and soft white clouds floated lazily overhead as the men settled themselves and lit cigarettes. On the special platform near the speakers stand, colonels and majors were a dime a dozen. Behind the platform stood Gen Patton's guard of honor, specially chosen men. At their right was the band playing rousing marches while the crowd waited and on the platform a nervous sergeant repeatedly tested the loudspeaker. The moment drew Nearer and necks craned to view the tiny winding road that led to Stourport-on-Severn..

"A captain stepped up to the microphone. 'When the generals arrive,' he said sonorously, 'the band will play the General's March and you will stand to attention.'

"By now the rumor had gotten around that Lt Gen Simpson, commanding the Fourth Army, was to be with Gen Patton. The men stirred expectantly - two of the big men in one day. At last the long black car, shining resplendently in the bright sun, roared up the road, preceded by a jeep full of MPs. A captain near the road turned and waved frantically and the men rose as one as a dead hush fell over the hillside. There he came. Impeccably dressed, with high boots and grim helmet, Patton strode down the incline and straight to the stiff-backed guard of honor. He looked them up and down, peered intently into their faces, surveyed their backs. He moved through the ranks of the statuesque band like an avenging wraith and, apparently satisfied, mounted the platform with Lt Gen Simpson and Maj Gen Cook, then corps commander.

"The Corps Chaplain gave the invocation, the men standing with bowed heads asking divine guidance for the great Third Army that they might speed victory to an enslaved Europe. Maj Gen Cook then introduced Lt Gen Simpson whose army was still in the United States, preparing for their own part in the war.

" 'We are here', said Gen Simpson,'to listen to the words of a great man, a man who will lead you all into whatever you may face with heroism, ability and foresight, a man who has proven himself amid shot and shell. My greatest hope is that some day I will have my own great army fighting with him, side by side.'

"Gen Patton arose and strode swiftly to the microphone, the men snapped to their feet and stood silently. Patton surveyed them grimly. 'Be seated.' The words were not a request but a command. The General's voice rose, high and clear:

" 'Men, this stuff we hear about America wanting to stay out of the war, not wanting to fight is a lot of bull......Americans love to fight - traditionally. All real Americans love the sting and clash of battle. When you were kids you admired the champion marble player, the fastest runner, the big league ball players, the toughest boxers. Americans play to win - all the time. I wouldn't give a hoot in hell for the man who lost and laughed. That's why Americans have never lost, nor never will lose a war, for the very thought of losing is hateful to an American ....' "

In the vein of this already widely known opening paragraph the general continued, his language growing more "colorful" by the minute. He left the men of XII Corps in no doubt as to exactly what he wanted them to help him do to the Germans. He went on to prescribe similar treatment for the Japs, and then assured his listeners that the shortest way home was through Berlin. He ended at the peak of his form on a highly modernized version of the St Crispin's Day speech by King Harry in Act IV of Henry the Fifth: "There is one thing you men will be able to say when you go home. You may all thank God for it. Thank God that at least thirty years from now when you are sitting around the fireside with your grandson on your knee and he asks you what you did in the great World War II you won't have to say: 'I shoveled shit in Louisiana!' "

And XII Corps legend has it that after Gen Patton had finished he turned to a certain officer on the stand near him, and said: "Well, Chaplain, did I make that rough enough for them?"

In spite of the long hours of work, and a 1030 pm curfew, life at Camp Bewdley also had its more frivolous aspects. Clubs were established, a PX was opened in the upper camp and one already open in the lower camp was taken over. A bus was laid on to the sales store at the Cheltenham S.O.S Headquarters. But most of the eyes in the camp were not turned to the usual facilities within any U.S Army installation. All around lay the "terra incognita" of beautiful and interesting countryside asking to be explored. Close at hand, on every side of the camp, was a friendly foreign people whose language was not so different from ours as to confuse simple issues. The contacts with these people for men of the XII Corps began with semi-official affairs: an exchange of parties with the Mayor and citizens of Kidderminster, other parties at Bewdley. There were organized tours to Leamington, Warwick Castle and Stratford-on-Avon, not far to the east of Bewdley. But very soon these official contacts gave way more to individual and highly unofficial relationships with the English.

XII Corps men walked and drove about through the countryside, learned the peculiarities of left-hand driving on narrow, traffic clogged roads beset by hedges and studded with blind corners. They also learned to whistle "Take the A Train", "The Jersey Bounce", "Tuxedo Junction", and to sing countless verses of "Lily from Piccadilly" and "Roll me over in the Clover". They located a favourite pub (e.g the "Stewpony" or "Chequers") and a favourite village, found out what a big tissue paper five pound note was worth in money, and visited with amiable ATS girls at the "Boars Nest" (sic) and with English families all around the neighbourhood.

Happy home though Camp Bewdley might have been for XII Corps, it was not to last forever. The camp had been designed for a hospital, and with D-Day and its casualties just around the corner, the medical people began to get all the hospitals they could ready for patients.

Informal records of the Corps reveal considerable regret at departing from Camp Bewdley, and even emotions more poignant than regret. "Great sadness because Bewdley would have been a nice place to sweat out the war .... ", "Many of us found Kidderminster and the rest of the countryside of England much better than we thought it would be, and had enjoyed our stay there. Some of us hated to leave ......".

On 15 June 1944, a week after D-Day, the Corps changed its Command Post location. Rumours running about the headquarters had it moving directly to all parts of the French coast that had been or might be invaded. The transfer turned out to be only about 20 miles into the city of Birmingham, but many felt that it was a long step, at least, down the road to the beach.

The Aggborough Football Ground was used by American servicemen stationed nearby for playing their national sport of baseball.

```
GRAND ALL-AMERICAN
   BASEBALL
      MATCH
Aggborough, Kidderminster
  Saturday, 15th April
  YANKEES v. REBELS
       First Strike 3.0 p.m.
       Gates open 2.15 p.m.
    Entrance to Ground 1/-, Stand
    1/- extra.
    (In   connection  with  A.T.C.
    Recruiting and Publicity Week).
                              161
```

Courtesy ; Kidderminster Shuttle

General George S. Patton, Jr. CG U.S Third Army visited Camp Bewdley twice during May 1944 to talk to the officers And men of the XII Corps.

Photo : Patton Museum of Cavalry and Armor

Major General Gilbert R. Cook is presented the Distinguished Service Medal by Major General James G. Christianson, Army War College.

Photo : National Archives

On 7 June 1944, a week before the departure of XII Corps, the following units were stationed at Bewdley Camp No.2 (Upper Camp):

>Headquarters XII Corps
>Headquarters Company XII Corps (with attached medical)
>XII Military Police Platoon
>Military Intelligence Team No.425
>Interrogation of Prisoners of War Team No.10
>Interrogation of Prisoners of War Team No.72
>Photo Interpreter Team No.52
>Detachment "YA" 21st Weather Squadron
>Detachment "YA" 40th Communication Squadron
>44th Machine Records Unit (Mobile) (Type Y)
>120th Army Postal Unit
>Headquarters XII Corps Artillery
>Headquarters Battery XII Corps Artillery
>93rd Signal Battalion
>9th Tank Destroyer Group
>Company "C" 511th Military Police Battalion

There were also advance detachments of the following units:

>Headquarters and Hq Battery 177th Field Artillery Group
>14th Field Artillery Observation Battalion
>191st Field Artillery Battalion (155mm Howitzer)
>689th Field Artillery Battalion (155mm Howitzer)

At Bewdley Camp No.1 (Lower Camp) the remaining units were as follows:

>3rd Auxiliary Surgical Group
>8th Armored Group Headquarters and Hq Company

The 2nd Cavalry Group and its associated Squadrons having departed to the south of England prior to embarkation to France.

Field Telephone Code Names

Combat units were given field telephone code names. The principal ones used at Camp Bewdley were :

>XII Corps ------------------ 'Iceberg'
>93rd Signal Battalion ----- 'Iceflow'
>511 MP Battalion ---------- 'Iceland'
>2nd Cavalry Group -------- 'Thoroughbred'
>2nd Cavalry Squadron ---- 'Hideout'
>42nd Cavalry Squadron --- 'Hidden'
>XII Corps Artillery -------- 'Idaho'

The following is an extract from the movement instructions issued for the move from Camp Bewdley to King Edward's School in Birmingham.

STAFF MEMORANDUM
NUMBER 11

>APO 312, U.S Army
>13 June 1944

ADMINISTRATIVE INSTRUCTIONS TO ACCOMPANY MOVEMENT ORDER NO. 5, HEADQUARTERS XII CORPS, DATED 12 JUNE 1944.

SECTION 1. Details of Movement.

1. Time.
This headquarters and attachments will begin movement to new CP at 0700, 15 June 1944.

2. Method.
Movement will be by motor.
  a. Trucks will be spotted at staff sections beginning at 0600, 15 June 1944 in accordance with attached schedule.
  b. Bicycles and other impedimenta will be loaded with section equipment and will move with the sections.
  c. C & R cars and 1/4 - ton trucks will be spotted at sections for transportation of officers beginning at 0800, 15 June 1944 in accordance with schedule to follow.
  d. Transportation Control Stations for vehicles will be established by the Motor Office, Headquarters Company, XII Corps at both the old and new CPs ....

3. Officers' Baggage.
Officers' Baggage will be tagged and ready for movement at 0800, 15 June 1944. The tags will show the officer's name, rank, serial number, and the number of the officer's quarters to which that officer is assigned. Tags will be distributed to officer's hutments by orderlies 13 June 1944.

4. Guides.
  a. Company "C" 511th MP Battalion will post guides at all critical intersections and traffic control points. They will post guides to indicate routes to billeting areas and officers' quarters.
  b. Strip maps of routes will be prepared by the Provost Marshal's Section and will be distributed to all drivers through the Transportation Officer, Headquarters Company, XII Corps.

5. Police.
All quarters and offices will be thoroughly policed prior to departure of personnel.

6. Rear Detachments.
  a. Transportation for rear detachments of sections will be spotted at Headquarters 0800, 16 June 1944.
  b. Headquarters Company, XII Corps will maintain rear detachment messing facilities throughout breakfast 16 June 1944.
  c. Rear detachments will mess at the present Headquarters Company enlisted men's mess.
  d. The Officer's Mess and the Enlisted Men's Mess at the new CP will be open for the noon meal 15 June 1944 .... "

Commanding Generals at Camp Bewdley 1943 -1944

Major General Emil F.Reinhardt   December 1943 - March 1944

    Was made Commanding General of VIII Corps in November 1943 at Brownwood, Texas, and accompanied the Corps on its move to the European Theater of Operations at Camp Bewdley, England. He left Camp Bewdley in March 1944 and returned to the United States. He assumed command of the 69th Infantry Division at Camp Shelby, Mississippi, in September 1944 and three months later returned to the European Theater of Operations with that division. On 25 April 1945, after a drive across Europe, advance units of his division made the initial contact with the Russian Army at the Elbe River.

Major General Troy H.Middleton   March 1944 - April 1944

    Assumed command of the 45th Infantry Division in October 1942. Accompanied this division overseas, serving in North Africa and Sicily. In January 1944 he returned to the United States and was assigned to Headquarters, Army Ground Forces, Washington, D.C. Two months later he assumed command of the VIII Corps at Camp Bewdley, England. He led the VIII Corps throughout the campaign in Europe.

Major General Gilbert R. Cook   April 1944 - June 1944

    Appointed Commanding General of the XII Corps in October 1943 at Fort Jackson, South Carolina, and conducted its training at Camp Forrest, Tennessee. He accompanied the Corps Headquarters on its move from Camp Forrest to Camp Bewdley, England. In addition to his other duties he was appointed Deputy Commander, Third Army in July 1944. He was in the Normandy and Northern France campaigns. He received the Distinguished Service Medal and the Croix de Guerre for his services.

Brigadier General John M. Lentz   April 1944 - June 1944

    Appointed Commander of the XII Corps Artillery on 5 February 1944 at Fort Jackson, South Carolina. He led the XII Corps Artillery throughout the campaign in Europe. Under his driving leadership the XII Corps Artillery was to play a tremendous part in the swift advances of the Corps and 3rd Army, and to be generally recognised as the most aggressive Artillery on the Western Front.

    While at Camp Bewdley he was the recipient of the Distinguished Service Medal.

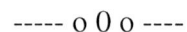

----- o O o ----

Generals visiting XII Corps at Camp Bewdley

27 April 1944
   Brigadier General H.L Earnest, 3rd Army Tank Destroyer Section Commander

8 May 1944
   Lt. General G.S Patton, Commanding General, 3rd Army

23 May 1944
   Major General Troy H Middleton, Commanding General, VIII Corps

31 May 1944
   Lt. General John C.H Lee, Commanding General , Services of Supply, ETOUSA
   Lt. General G.S Patton, Commanding General, 3rd Army
   Lt. General W.H Simpson, Commanding General, 4th Army
   Brigadier General James E Moore, Chief of Staff, 4th Army

1 June 1944
   Lt. General W.H Simpson, Commanding General, 4th Army
   Brigadier General James E Moore, Chief of Staff, 4th Army
   Major General J. Leclerc, 2nd French Armored Division Commander

5 June 1944
   Major General L.E Oliver, Commanding General, 5th Armored Division
   Brigadier General Regnier.

------ o O o ------

93rd Signal Battalion

Extracts from the 93rd Signal Battalion History

Early on the morning of 18 April 1944 Major Scanlon and nine other officers departed from Camp Shanks to serve as "loading officers" and after an interesting ride on a river steamer were overjoyed to learn that the huge "Queen Elizabeth" would be the ship to take us across the seas. The balance of the Battalion boarded the ship the night of the 19th and in the early morning fog of the 20th the "Good Queen Liz" nosed her way out of New York Harbor. It seemed that everyone aboard the ship was awake to take that last look at the Statue of Liberty which was faintly discernible at that hour.

After an uneventful voyage which found all members of the outfit in good shape .... everyone was overjoyed at the first landfall about 0900 in the morning of the 26th and all aboard were on deck to watch the passage of the picturesque shores of the Firth of Clyde. The "Lizzie" dropped anchor about the middle of the afternoon and at a conference that evening it was learned that half the Battalion had been designated to be the first unit to unload next morning.

We were treated to a ride on the train past Glasgow and down through the midlands of England to the little station of Bewdley. There at the station we were met by members of our advance party and Capt Myers, Assistant Signal Officer of XII Corps. The first section of the Battalion to arrive at Camp Bewdley made adequate preparations for the arrival of the second half the following night.

The most difficult part of our preparations for combat that were carried out in England was the drawing of our full TBA equipment. Because of the threat of aerial bombardment Army Service Forces had established depots throughout the British Isles and many long trips were made before all of the equipment allotted to the Battalion was on hand. In the meantime the Operations Company personnel had an opportunity to become acquainted with the Corps Headquarters and its methods of operations because they operated the switchboard for the Camp as well as Teletypewriter service and Message Center facilities. Our Messengers soon became adept at driving on the "wrong" side of the road and learned to laugh at the Englishman's never failing "You cawn't miss it" when they inquired directions.

All personnel soon became acquainted with the British pubs and sighed at the short supply of Scotch. Pass policies were liberal and everyone took advantage of the fact to get acquainted with the lads and lassies, mostly the latter!

We were sadly disappointed when orders came that Camp Bewdley must be vacated in favour of a hospital unit, and it was with much misgivings that we moved to Camp Coton, a tent camp, located on the rolling hills about ten miles north of Kidderminster. It was at Camp Coton that we first became acquainted with the famed (or is it infamous) English "honey buckets". At the same time that the Battalion moved to Camp Coton the Corps Headquarters moved to Birmingham and an Operating Detachment of personnel from the Message Center Telephone and Teletype platoons was sent along to care for the Corps' communication requirements.

Unit strength: 31 Officers
1 Warrant Officer
897 Enlisted Men

3rd Auxiliary Surgical Group

APO 651 Telephone No. : Stourport 370

Arrived at Bewdley (Lower Camp) 21 December 1943 per Western Base Section Movement Order No.501.
Strength of unit :
132 Officers
70 Nurses
176 Enlisted Men

Organization of Auxiliary Surgical Group

Headquarters : 3 Officers, 2 Nurses, 51 Enlisted Men

24 Surgical Teams consisting of :
    1 General Surgeon
    1 Assistant General Surgeon
    1 Anesthetist
    1 Nurse
    2 Surgical Technicians

6 Orthopedic Teams consisting of :
    1 Orthopedic Surgeon
    1 Nurse
    2 Surgical Technicians

6 Shock Teams consisting of :
    1 General Surgeon
    1 Nurse
    2 Surgical Technicians

6 Gas Teams consisting of :
    1 Officer specially trained in treatment of chemical casualties
    2 Nurses
    2 Medical Technicians

4 Maxillo-facial Teams consisting of :
    1 Plastic Surgeon
    1 Oral Surgeon
    1 Nurse Anesthetist
    1 Nurse
    1 Dental Technician
    1 Surgical Technician

4 Neuro-surgical Teams consisting of
    1 Neuro-surgeon
    1 Assistant Operating Surgeon
    1 Anesthetist
    1 Nurse
    2 Surgical Technicians

4 Thoracic-surgical Teams consisting of :
    1 Thoracic Surgeon
    1 Assistant Surgeon
    1 Anesthetist (intra-trachial)
    1 Nurse
    2 Surgical Technicians

3 Dental-prosthetic Teams consisting of :
    1 Prosthetist
    3 Dental Technicians

3 Cars, 5 passenger, light sedan
1 Truck, 3/4 ton , weapon carrier
2 Trucks, 1 1/2 ton, cargo
3 Trucks, 2 1/2 ton dental laboratory

Approximate date of departure of 3rd Auxiliary Surgical Group from Camp Bewdley : 1 August 1944.

9th Tank Destroyer Group

The unit staged through Camp Kilmer and departed from New York Port of Embarkation on 3rd May 1944 on the SS Highland Monarch, as part of a 60 ship convoy, for a 13 day trip to Avonmouth Port, England. They went directly to Camp Bewdley and were assigned to XII Corps.

The 9th T.D Group watched over the XII T.D Battalions. Its Commanding Officer, Colonel Lansing McVickar, was extremely popular and well acquainted among personnel of the Corps staff. When he was later killed in the Bulge fighting it was widely felt that although his name does not appear in the Corps Headquarters rosters a regular member of the staff had been lost.

On 18th June 1944 the group moved by motor convoy from Camp Bewdley to Moseley Village, Birmingham.

Unit strength: 15 Officers
61 Enlisted Men

1st Tank Destroyer Brigade

APO 230   Telephone No: Stourport 370 Extension 2001

Arrived Bewdley 31 January 1944

Departed for Macclesfield 5 April 1944

Unit strength: 8 Officers
53 Enlisted Men

8th Armored Group

APO 308

Arrived Camp Bewdley 24 February 1944

Departed July 1944 for Utah beach

Unit strength: 17 Officers
1 Warrant Officer
87 Enlisted Men

2nd Cavalry Group (Mecz)
2nd Cavalry Squadron (Mecz)
42nd Cavalry Squadron (Mecz)

Unit strength:

    Group Headquarters: 15 Officers
                                    57 Enlisted Men
    2nd Cavalry Squadron: 39 Officers
                                    2 Warrant Officers
                                    733 Enlisted Men
    42nd Cavalry Squadron: 38 Officers
                                    3 Warrant Officers
                                    733 Enlisted Men

    Total: 92 Officers
                 1523 Enlisted Men
                 5 Warrant Officers

Extracts from Daily Diary

10 April 1944
At 0730, Group Headquarters and Headquarters Troop departed New York Harbor on the unescorted troop transport "Queen Mary" for the unannounced port in Scotland. Due to the number of troops on board, only two meals per day were served. Lifeboat drill held each morning. Lectures on pertinent military subjects given to Group Headquarters Troop by the Troop C.O.

16 April 1944
"Queen Mary" arrived Clyde River, Scotland, 2100 and anchored off Greenock

17 April 1944
Group Hqs and Hqs Troop disembarked from the "Queen Mary" and proceeded to Greenock to board train for Camp Bewdley, Worcestershire, England. Left Greenock at 1600.

18 April 1944
Group Hqs and Hqs Troop, after all night journey, arrived Camp Bewdley, England at 0645 and were met by the two officers who had preceded Group as the advance party. Billets were assigned and the various sections prepared to start operations.

19 April 1944
Group Hqs and Hqs Troop made preparations to draw various necessary supplies and reconnoitered for areas to accommodate Squadrons upon their arrival.

20 April 1944
    2nd Cavalry Squadron departed Camp Kilmer, 0700 for POE New York. Arrived Jersey City 1000, immediately boarded ferry and proceeded to the embarkation pier arriving 1200. Upon arrival boarded the troop transport "Mauretania".

21 April 1944
    42nd Cavalry Squadron departed Camp Kilmer, 1900 for POE New York, arriving 2030, thence proceeded to ferry to the embarkation pier, arriving 2130. Upon arrival joined the 2nd Cavalry Squadron on board the "Mauretania".

22 April 1944
    2nd Cavalry Squadron and 42nd Cavalry Squadron departed New York Harbor 0500 for Liverpool, England, on board the "Mauretania"

19 -30 April 1944
    Group Hqs and Hqs Troop on routine garrison duties at Camp Bewdley.

30 April 1944
    2nd and 42nd Cavalry Squadrons arrived Liverpool and docked at 0600. Departed Liverpool by train at 1800 for Camp Bewdley.

1 May 1944
    Representatives from Group Hqs and Hqs Troop met the 2nd and 43nd Cavalry Squadrons upon their arrival at Camp Bewdley, and assisted in the billetting of the various troops. The Squadron Commanders and their officers were orientated in rules and regulations governing the new area.

2 May 1944
    The troops made various improvements in their respective areas to increase the comfort of the men. Squadron S-3s (Operations) drew up training schedules. One of the main subjects stressed was physical training. At least three road marches per week were scheduled. Squadron S-4s (Supply) started requisitioning necessary equipment to prepare their Squadrons for combat.

3-15 May
    Usual training duties. On 10 May Group Headquarters assigned a telephone number - Stourport 370, Extension 176.

16 May 1944
    Both the 2nd and 42nd Squadrons were divided into forward and rear echelons and alerted for movement.

17 May 1944
    The forward echelons of the Squadrons were further divided into two parts, and orders were received to move on 18 May 1944.

18 May 1944

Both sections of the forward echelon of 2nd Cavalry departed Camp Bewdley by rail. Destination of the first section was Torquay, while the second section departed for Plymouth.

Both sections of the forward echelon of 42nd Cavalry departed Camp Bewdley by rail. Destination of the first section was Dorchester, and the second section departed for Glen Eyre (Southampton Marshalling Area).

All movements were made per authority Telegram Message, Headquarters Third US Army, Dated 16 May 1944, Movement Orders No.57.

The forward echelons of both squadrons were moved to the above named places to assist the transient troops in their passage thru the Marshalling Area. Group Hq and both the Squadron Rear Echelons remained at Camp Bewdley performing usual training duties.

25 May 1944

Group Headquarters and Hq Troop and Squadron rear echelons departed Camp Bewdley, by road, starting 0730, per authority Movement Orders No.57, Headquarters Third US Army dated 16 May 1944, as amended by VOCG Southern Base Section, Services of Supply, European Theater of Operations, US Army.

Arrived Camp Fargo, Larkhill, Wiltshire, England, 1600 hours.

3345 QM Truck Company (clrd)

APO 308   Telephone No. Stourport 370 Ext 157

Unit strength : 5 Officers   110 Enlisted men.

Arrived Bewdley 21 March 1944.
Departed 4 May 1944 to Mumbles, Glamorgan

3326 QM Truck Company (clrd)

Unit strength : 5 Officers   110 Enlisted men.

3516 Ordnance Medical Auto Maint Company

Unit strength : 4 Officers   112 Enlisted men

Arrived Bewdley March 1944
Departed 27 April 1944 to Arrow Park, Cheshire.

Photo : Kenneth Wakefield
Piper L - 4 Liaison plane

Liaison Aircraft

The VIII and XII Corps, while at Camp Bewdley, each had the use of two liaison aircraft, the landing strip being in a field adjacent to the Upper Camp. Two liaison pilots were assigned to each Corps.

The most widely used liaison aircraft was the Piper L-4 powered by a 65hp Continental 0-170-3 (A-65) engine. Although officially called the Grasshopper, it was invariably known as the Cub, the name of the almost identical civilian light plane from which it was developed.

Also used was the heavier Stinson L-5 Sentinel, powered by a Lycoming 0-435-1 engine.

They were employed on courier duties, mail runs, general communications and administrative flights.

Weather and Communication Squadrons

Weather and Communication Squadrons of the 9th Air Force were attached to the Corps Headquarters to provide general weather information

The Weather Squadron to make observations and give briefings. The Communications Squadron, consisting of wireless operators to carry out associated radio and teletype communications, mainly weather data to and from other stations.

In addition to their primary task of advising Corps Commanders and their staffs on weather matters, forecasts were given to the Corps Headquarters Air Section, and to the air sections of Divisions and Battalions assigned hereto. Of particular importance were warnings of high winds and snow, both of which could seriously damage light liaison aircraft parked in the open, as they invariably were. Forewarned they could be tied down securely or otherwise protected.

Bewdley Camp No.1 (Lower Camp)
Detachment Mess in the foreground, Medical Wards are in the background. Burlish Crossing is on the left of the photograph. The train would have been the early afternoon service from Hartlebury to Shrewsbury.

Bewdley Camp No.1 (Lower Camp)
Administration Building in the centre foreground with the Surgical Wards behind. Burlish Crossing is to the right of this photograph.
Both photos by Sergeant John P.Thomson (John Harper collection)

THE HOSPITALS

The 12th Medical Hospital Center

On 8 March 1944 an organisation known as the 12th Medical Hospital Center, under the command of Colonel Lehman, arrived at Swansea Docks after an eleven day sea voyage from New York. The following day the unit disembarked and entrained for its new station in the United Kingdom at Great Malvern, arriving in the early hours of 11 March 1944 with 30 Officers, 3 Warrant Officers and 227 Enlisted Men.

The function of the 12th Medical Hospital Center was to act as a headquarters for a group of hospitals in Worcestershire and Herefordshire, seven of which were already active at this time serving the needs of the numerous U.S Army Units stationed in the area.

Those hospitals already in operation were located at the following sites:

- Blackmore Park Camp No.1   Nr Malvern Wells
- Blackmore Park Camp No.2   Nr Malvern Wells
- Brickbarns   Malvern Wells
- Wood Farm   Malvern Wells
- Merebrook Farm   Malvern Wells
- Wolverley   Nr Kidderminster
- Barons Cross   Leominster

With the advent of D-Day a further six General Hospitals were due to be activated and attached to the 12th Medical Hospital Center. These were to be set up at Dual Purpose Camps after the departure of the combat troops who had been using these camps prior to landing in Normandy.

The camps involved were:

    Bewdley Camp No.1
    Bewdley Camp No.2
    Kington Camp No.1
    Kington Camp No.2
    Foxley Camp No.1   Nr Hereford
    Foxley Camp No.2   Nr Hereford

The 12th Medical Hospital Center was responsible for the allotment of casualties from the invasion of France to the General Hospitals under its control. All administrative duties connected with the reception and evacuation of patients being co-ordinated and controlled by the Center.

65 ambulances and 6 requisitioned London buses were allocated to the Center for the evacuation of patients. The buses were a decided advantage in the evacuation of ambulatory patients, although continuous repair work was necessary to maintain the performance of the vehicles.

The main source of admission of patients to the hospitals was by hospital train (known as train convoy) from:

    (a) Transit hospitals near ports or airfields in the south of England.
    (b) Southampton Docks

Disposition of patients after treatment was either to:

    (a) 10th Replacement Depots at Lichfield and Pheasey Farm, Birmingham
    (b) Convalescent Hospitals at Stoneleigh, Packington or Bromsgrove
    (c) Zone of Interior (U.S.A) via a holding hospital at Malvern
    (d) Duty

Special ceremonies were held at the hospitals for the awards of Purple Hearts and Oak Leaf Clusters.

The Purple Heart, a decoration for valor, was awarded to patients for wounds received in action against an enemy of the United States.

The Purple Heart consisted of a bronze bust on a purple background surrounded by a bronze border, surmounted by a shield with red stars and bars on a white background with, on either side, green leaves. The ribbon was purple edged in white.

Oak Leaf Clusters were awarded for further wounds received in action.

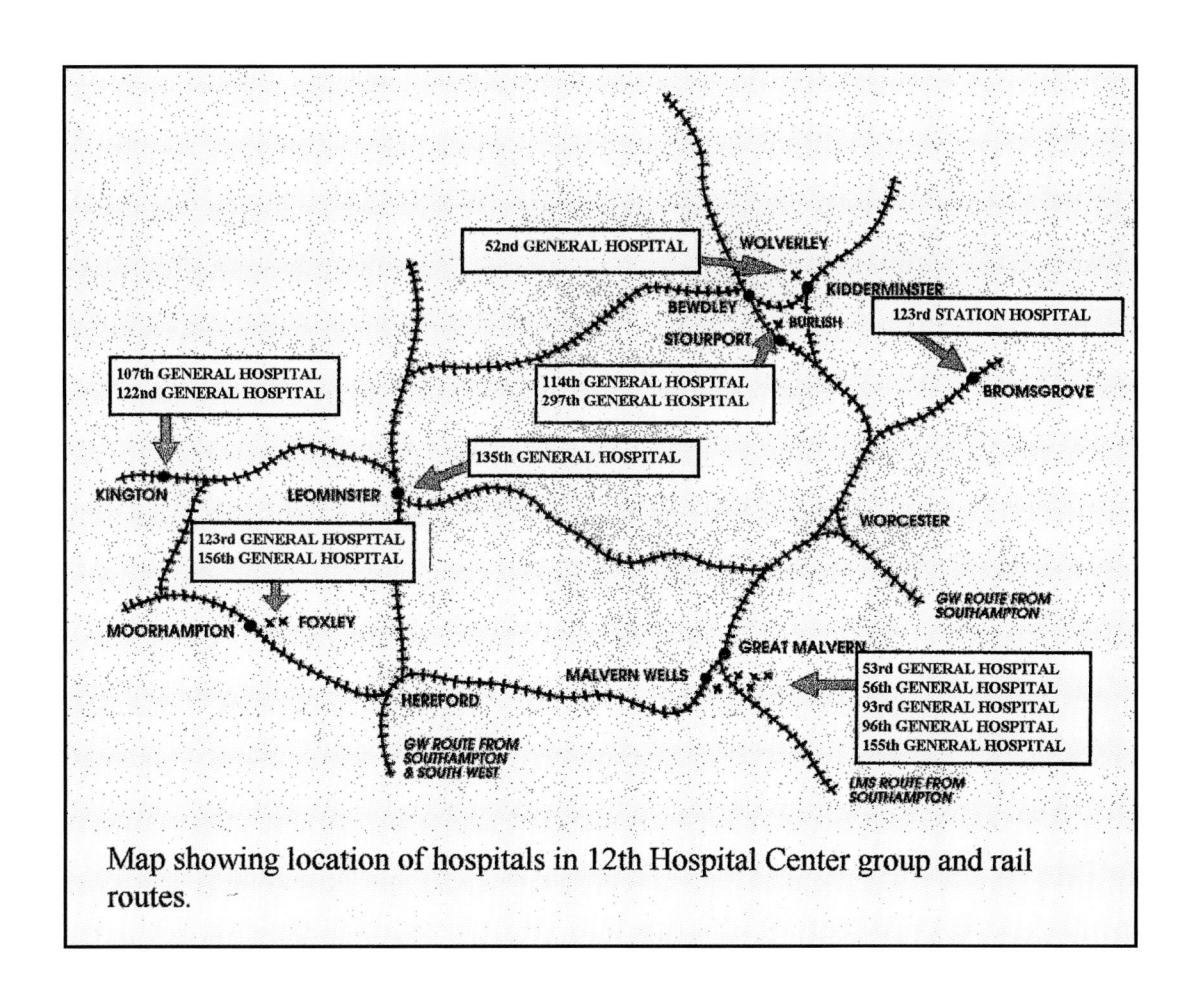

Map showing location of hospitals in 12th Hospital Center group and rail routes.

Hospital Plant No.	Hospital Unit	Site	Bed Capacity
4168	123SH	Bromsgrove	400
4169	52GH	Wolverley	1534
4170	297GH	Bewdley No.1	1442
4171	114GH	Bewdley No.2	1442
4172	93GH	Blackmore Park	1459
4173	155GH	Blackmore Park	1367
4174	96GH	Brickbarns	1427
4175	53GH	Merebrook Farm	1517
4176	55GH	Wood Farm	1517
4177	135GH	Barons Cross	1164
4178	123GH	Foxley No.1	1442
4179	156GH	Foxley No.2	1442
4180	122GH	Kington No.1	1442
4181	107GH	Kington No.2	1442

The American Red Cross

Five American Red Cross workers were assigned to each hospital. Two were recreation workers, two were social workers and one was a secretary. Their function was to co-ordinate and conduct a welfare programme for the patients in close co-operation with the medical authorities, and to perform welfare services for the Medical Detachment, Officers and Nurses.

The recreation work services offered by the American Red Cross, assisted by the local Red Cross and volunteers, entertained patients on the wards and in the recreation halls. The entertainment consisted of :
- (a) movies
- (b) parties
- (c) art and craft classes
- (d) theatre parties
- (e) Doughnutmobile and travelling entertainments

The social work services offered, in close teamwork with the Medical Officers and Nurses, fell into the following categories:
1. Family problems, marital and other.
2. Adjustments to illness, both physical and mental.
    - (a) Personal and social information gathered for Medical Officers as an aid in diagnosis and treatment.
    - (b) Understanding and acceptance of their physical conditions to facilitate willing co-operation with medical treatment.
    - (c) Help in facing and accepting physical conditions entailing permanent disabilities.
    - (d) Medical and social interpretation of the patient's condition to families through the Home Chapters.
3. Adjustment in attitude towards the Army.
    Help in resolving fears and resistance to return to duty and active combat.
4. Financial help.

In addition to the above professional Social Work Service the American Red Cross assisted patients physically or emotionally unable to write letters home.

The Hospital Buildings

Each hospital plant comprised of over 120 buildings of a semi-permanent type.
Ward buildings were of wooden construction.
Clinics, laboratories and mess halls were for the most part of brick construction.
Officers and Nurses quarters were huts of wooden construction, each housing four to eight per hut.

Detachment barracks were of wooden construction, each housing approximately 30 men.

Officers quarters, nurses quarters and Enlisted Men's barracks were each served by respective centrally located latrines including shower room. Hot water was provided by boilers in each latrine. A central boiler plant provided steam for the Operating Room and Central Supply, and hot water for the Surgical Wards. A second boiler plant provided hot water for the Medical Wards. All other heating throughout the installations was provided by small coal burning stoves.

The wards were of British design and contained Kitchen, latrine, shower room, linen room, office and examining room. Each ward contained approximately three private rooms, the remainder of the ward being devoted to open bed space.

The plant buildings comprised the following:

>Headquarters Building
>Guard House
>Receiving and Evacuation Office
>Information Office
>Mortuary
>Post Office
>PX Exchange
>Boiler House
>Fire House
>Red Cross Office
>Chapel
>Pharmacy
>Dispensary
>X-Ray Clinic
>Laboratory
>Dental Clinic
>E.E.N.T
>36 Ward Buildings
>18 Nurses' Quarters
>13 Officers' Quarters
>Detachment Office
>19 Enlisted Men's Barracks
>Officers' Mess Hall
>Detachment Mess Hall
>Officer Patient's Mess Hall
>Patient's Mess Hall
>4 Latrines
>Central Supply Office
>Medical Supply Office
>Unit Supply Office
>Officers Club
>Enlisted Men's Recreation Room
>Patient's Recreation Room

297th General Hospital

The hospital unit was activated on 10 June 1943 at Temple, Texas as an affiliated unit of Cook County Hospital, Chicago, Illinois. On 22 March 1944 the unit moved to Fort Dix, New Jersey. During the stay at Fort Dix, a full time training programme of all personnel for overseas service was in progress.

On 24 May 1944 the organisation proceeded by motor convoy to Camp Kilmer, New Jersey. At Camp Kilmer, the final processing for embarkation was completed, and replacements were received for three enlisted men AWOL. The organisation arrived at Kilmer at noon on Wednesday and embarked at New York harbour on the following Monday night, 29 May 1944. Debarkation was made at Gourock, Scotland on 6 June 1944, and the organisation immediately boarded the train and proceeded to Llandudno, North Wales.

Llanduduno proved to be a provisional hospital training area. A headquarters was established in a rented civilian building, and the organisation obtained billets in semi-private hotels or rooming places throughout the town. Mess was taken at centrally located army messes in Nissen huts, one for officers and nurses and one for the enlisted men. A full time training programme was carried out while the organisation remained at this location pending assignment to the installation which it was to operate.

On 19 June 1944, the entire organisation proceeded by rail to Camp Bewdley, Stourport, Worcestershire to take over an existing building plant designated and designed for operation as a hospital.

The camp or post at Bewdley included two hospital plant structures of British construction, the "lower" camp, later designated as Hospital Plant 4170 and the "upper" camp, later designated as Hospital Plant 4171. This organisation took over the occupancy of the lower camp, Plant 4170, and immediately proceeded to prepare the plant for operation as a General Hospital. The plant site had just recently been evacuated by Ground Force troops who had utilized the plant for billets. British civilian contractors were at work renovating and making alterations to the plant to prepare for its proper function as a hospital. Considerable construction, renovation and alteration was required before the hospital was ready, on 17 July 1944, to receive patients.

Fourteen hundred and forty two beds were set up in the installation, and the organisation was ready to handle that number of patients without expansion beyond fixed facilities. During the period from 19 June to 17 July 1944, while the plant was undergoing repair, an extensive training programme was carried out embracing:

    Chemical Warfare
    Messing and Nutrition in the ETO
    Military Courtesy
    Physical Conditioning
    Bomb Reconnaissance
    Fire Fighting
    Review of Technical Training

Files of current ETO directives had been obtained and were reviewed by the Commanding Officer with all commissioned personnel.

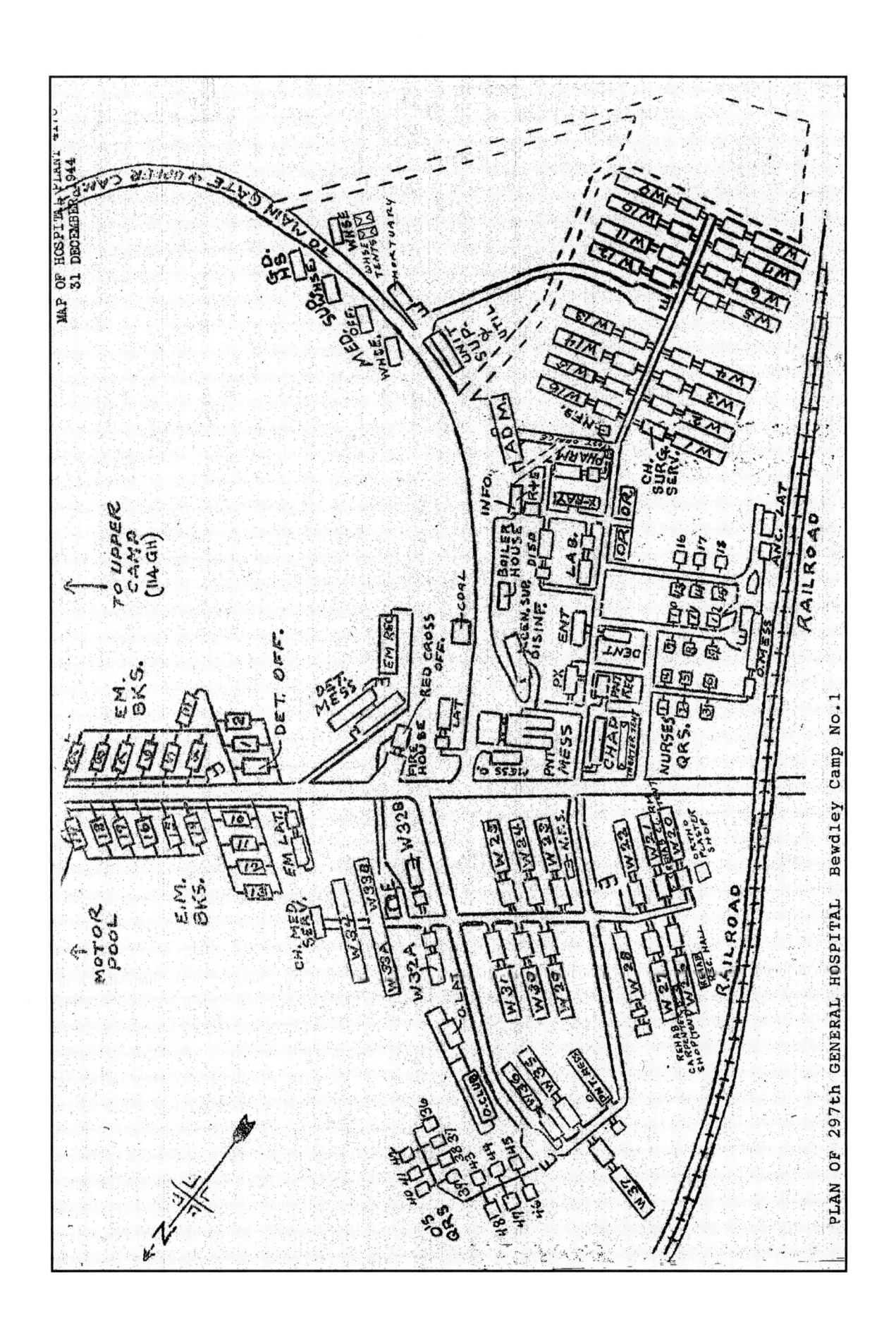

PLAN OF 297th GENERAL HOSPITAL Bewdley Camp No. 1

Organisation of 297 General Hospital   19 July 1944

ADMINISTRATIVE

> Commanding Officer .... Col. Francis W Pruitt
> Executive Officer .... Major Gordon E Snyder
> Adjutant .... 1st Lt. Howard E Stingel
> Assistant Adjutant .... CWO Otis L McKoy
> Registrar .... Capt Lee Jarvis
> Receiving and Evacuation Officer .... Capt Lee Jarvis
> C.O Detachment of Patients .... 1st Lt. Armin R Molin
> C.O Medical Detachment .... Major Lawrence A Levitin
> Special Service Officer .... 1st Lt. James N White
> Provost Marshal . ... 1st Lt. Ernest V Smith
> Fire Marshal .... 2nd Lt. Sydney S Levine
> Chief of Nursing Service .... Major Loree Wolf
> Mess Officer .... Capt Francis J Werner
> Dietetic Service .... 1st Lt Mary F Nusbaum
> Utility Officer .... 2nd Lt. Marlin A Peterson
> Medical and Unit Supply Officer .... Capt Clifford G Benson
> Personnel Officer .... 1st Lt. James N White
> Protestant Chaplain .... Capt Waldo S Richards
> Catholic Chaplain .... Capt Leo J Garvey

PROFESSIONAL

> Medical Service .... Lt Col. George F O'Brien
>> Acute Infectious Section .... Major Melvin L Afremow
>> Cardio-Vascular Renal Section .... Major John Ashworth
>> Neuropsychiatric Section .... Major Lawrence A Levitin
>> Gastro Intestinal Section .... Major Emmett D Wall
>> General Medicine Section .... Major Paul L Bedringer
>> Dermatology Section .... Capt Leonard D Trilling
>
> Surgical Service .... Lt Col Chester C Guy
>> Urological Section .... Major Peter A Nelson
>> Orthopedic Section .... Major Hampar Kelikian
>> E.E.N.T Section .... Major John J Walsh
>> General Surgery Section .... Major William C Beck
>> Neuro Surgery Section .... Major Wesley A Gustafson
>
> Roentgenological Service .... Lt Col Elbert K Lewis
> Central Supply Department .... 1st Lt Helen Darper
> Pharmacy .... 1st Lt Armin R Molin
> Dental Service .... Lt Col Joseph L Ubl
> Laboratory Service .... Lt Col Alex B Ragins
> Physical Therapy .... 1st Lt Nadine Coyne
> Rehabilitation .... Major Max Kaplan

Strength of Organisation on arrival in U.K:

56 Officers
1 Warrant Officer
83 Nurses
3 Hospital Dietitians
3 Physical Therapists
5 Red Cross Workers
500 Enlisted Men

On 19 July 1944 the first convoy of patients was received by train from the 315th Station Hospital at Axminster. The convoy consisted of 293 patients of whom 228 were litter cases. The patients almost entirely were battle casualties, surgical cases, very recently evacuated from the Normandy, France area.

Convoys by train from other hospitals in the south of England were received on 23 July, 28 July and 2 August. By 15 August the census of the hospital had reached a total of 1,289 patients.

During the period of the first years operations there were over 7,570 admissions, or an average total of approximately 630 patients each month. Over 7,000 patients had been disposed of up to the beginning of June 1945 as follows:

Discharged to Duty 2,375
Transferred to other hospitals 2,154
Transferred for Z.I (U.S.A) 2,460

Other than U.S Army personnel treated at this hospital consisted of :

U.S Navy 6
British 27
Free French 26
Canadian 2
U.S Merchant Marine 1
Italian Co-operative 1
Total 69

Of the total patients received at this hospital all were transferred here for further observation and treatment, with the exception of 268 U.S Army personnel received during May 1945 as holding patients for Z.I until evacuation could be arranged.

In all, during the first year of operations, 26 cases were reported as seriously ill, including 24 battle casualties and 2 non-battle casualties. Four of these seriously ill cases terminated in death, and 24 of these cases recovered. The average time a patient remained on the seriously ill list was nine days.

Patients were permitted passes from the hospital after they had become ambulatory and after they had been here fifteen days. This permitted them to visit neighbouring towns between the hours of 1.00pm and 9.30pm. In some instances, where friends or relatives of patients were located in the U.K, 24 or 48 hour passes were granted.

While there were a number of violations under these privileges, on the whole the members of the Detachment of Patients conducted themselves remarkably well, and with credit to the installation and themselves.

At the Information Desk a control register was kept on visitors to patients in the hospital. Visiting hours were restricted to between the hours of 2pm and 4pm, in order not to conflict with the care and attention required by the patients. In all, a total of 3,568 civilians visited the patients in the hospital. Every effort was made to make the stay of patients as pleasant as possible.

Civilian Personnel

The following civilian personnel were performing necessary maintenance work at the time this organisation moved to this station on 19 June 1944:

1 Foreman   1 Plumber
1 Fitter   6 Stokers
1 Carpenter   1 Labourer

By the end of July 1944 this had increased to:

1 Foreman   1 Pump attendant   5 Labourers
1 Electrician   1 Plumber   2 Seamstresses
1 Fitter   1 Boiler attendant   12 Cleaners
1 Carpenter   6 Stokers

At the end of April 1945 the civilians employed were as follows:

1 Foreman   1 Plumber   5 Labourers
1 Electrician   1 Pump attendant   1 Shorthand typist
1 Fitter   2 Boiler attendants   3 Telephone operators
1 Carpenter   6 Stokers   3 Seamstresses
                                         14 Cleaners

Enlisted Men's Recreational Activities

For the entertainment of the enlisted personnel regular scheduled leagues consisting of baseball, softball, volley ball and basketball were set up by the Special Services Department. These activities created considerable interest among the men and kept them occupied during their off duty hours.

<u>Baseball</u>
The 297 Baseball Team was considered to be one of the finest in the district. Permission was secured from the Steatite Porcelain Works Ltd to lay out a baseball diamond on their cricket field. The result was a very fine baseball diamond. A backstop was built, the diamond rolled and levelled and the grass cut. Outfitted completely with the finest

equipment the department could procure, the baseball team provided hours of pleasure and enjoyment to many.

Softball

The unit was a member of the 12th Hospital Center Softball League (Northern) and was victorious in three engagements while losing two.

Victories were scored against:
- 826th Convalescent Center (Stoneleigh)
- 52nd General Hospital (Wolverley)
- 114th General Hospital (Bewdley Upper Camp)

The two defeats were against:
- 825th Convalescent Center (Packington Hall)

Inter barrack softball games were played during the season (April until August) on Tuesday and Thursday evenings and Saturday afternoons. The teams were named as follows:

Barracks		Barracks	
2 and 3	Bears	12 and 13	Mustangs
4 and 5	Terriers	14 and 15	Wildcats
6 and 7	Wolves	16 and 17	Panthers
8 and 9	Scroungers	18 and 19	Tigers
10 and 11	Greyhounds		

Basketball

The basketball team was coached and managed by S/Sgt Joseph Derrickson. Home games were played at the Kidderminster Baths.

Teams played included:

- G25 (Ashchurch)
- 52nd General Hospital (Wolverley)
- 93rd General Hospital (Malvern)
- 96th General Hospital (Malvern)
- 825th Convalescent Center (Packington Hall)
- 826th Convalescent Center (Stoneleigh)
- 833rd Convalescent Center (Bromsgrove)

Volleyball

Volleyball games were played on Monday, Wednesday and Friday evenings. Teams were as follows:
1. Medical Supply
2. Rehabilitation
3. Barracks No.10
4. Motor Pool
5. Personnel
6. Detachment Office
7. Laboratory

The Post Theatre

The Post Theatre Tent was constructed to provide a central meeting place which could accommodate a large number of personnel, and was used mainly for the showing of movies and training films. Movies were shown three evenings a week, Tuesdays, Fridays and Sundays. The attendance at these sessions was usually very high, attesting to the popularity of movies on the Post. From time to time as the occasion arose, the Tent was also used to hold various meetings, Purple Heart ceremonies and civilian speakers.

As time went on, it was felt that a more substantial building was needed , so lumber and supplies were obtained and wooden sides were built onto the tent to reduce draught. The center poles were later removed from the tent and it was strung on cable from telephone poles thus giving clearer vision and increasing the seating capacity to 500. Cement blocks were laid on the cinder floor and this added considerably to the comfort of the tent. These blocks, as was much of the material used in improving the tent were obtained from abandoned sites throughout the district and with permission of the British Goverment.

Next was the construction of the stage which was used for various attractions and stage shows. Dressing rooms and a projection room were also constructed. The stage was equipped with Special Service material and was considered to be one of the finest in the district and received much favourable comment from the performers.

U.S.O Shows

Special Service assumed all responsibility for all U.S.O shows presented at this installation. Accompanying the transportation from the pick up point back to the post, the members of the troupe were under the supervision of Special Service non-commissioned officers at all times. The Special Service Officer met all incoming shows and stayed until their departure.

Civilian Shows

From time to time civilian shows were booked for this post. These shows offered a cross section of English humour and were greatly enjoyed. Usually several of the performers were great artists in the theatrical world and musical world in England and were attached to these units playing army camps in the U.K.

C.E.M.A Concerts

The Committee for the Encouragement of the Musical Arts usually presented this department with at least one concert a month. They catered mainly to the wards throughout the hospital, reaching the bed patients who could not attend shows at the Post Theatre.

Radio Station

Daily radio broadcasts were given by the Special Services reporter. Details of shows, plays, concerts, local movies and other pertinent information was announced for the convenience of patients and personnel.

Speakers were installed in wards, mess halls and departments throughout the hospital. This proved to be highly successful in bringing to patients and personnel news and radio programs during the day and evening.

Outside Visits

Plays
     Personnel were given the opportunity of attending plays presented throughout the area, including the Stratford Memorial Theatre, where many of Shakespeare's plays were enjoyed, and the Theatre Royal in Worcester where some very fine plays were presented each week and regular trips were taken.

Sight Seeing Tours
     With the co-operation of the British Council in Birmingham, sight seeing tours to Stratford upon Avon and Kenilworth Castle were a regular monthly feature for patients and personnel of the post. The Red Cross assumed all responsibility for the procuring of patients for these trips.

Glass Factory Trips
     Trips were taken to the Stourbridge Glass Factory where the various methods of producing and manufacturing glassware were observed. Trips of this type were greatly encouraged for a work of art in glassware is seldom seen.

Birmingham Town Hall Concerts
     The Special Services Department reserved bookings and arranged transport to various concerts which were presented in nearby communities.
     The Town Hall, Birmingham offered the following:

Friday, 16 February 1945 .... The London Philharmonic Orchestra
Tuesday, 27 February 1945 ..... The Liverpool Philharmonic Orchestra
Tuesday, 13 March 1945 .... The London Philharmonic Orchestra
Monday, 26 March 1945 .... The Liverpool Philharmonic Orchestra
Tuesday, 10 April 1945 .... The London Philharmonic Orchestra
Tuesday, 17 April 1945 .... The Halle Orchestra

Swimming Parties
     Regular swimming parties were held at the Stourbridge Baths each Wednesday evening.

Bus Service
     A bus service was established between the hospital and the town of Kidderminster, approximately 3 miles away. A truck left the Receiving Office each hour starting at 1815 until 2215 hours. A guard was detailed each night to ride the truck and check passes and see that order was maintained. One truck also made one trip to the town of Stourbridge and back each night for the Detachment men, a distance of approximately 11 miles. The driver was furnished on a voluntary basis and was not detailed by roster.

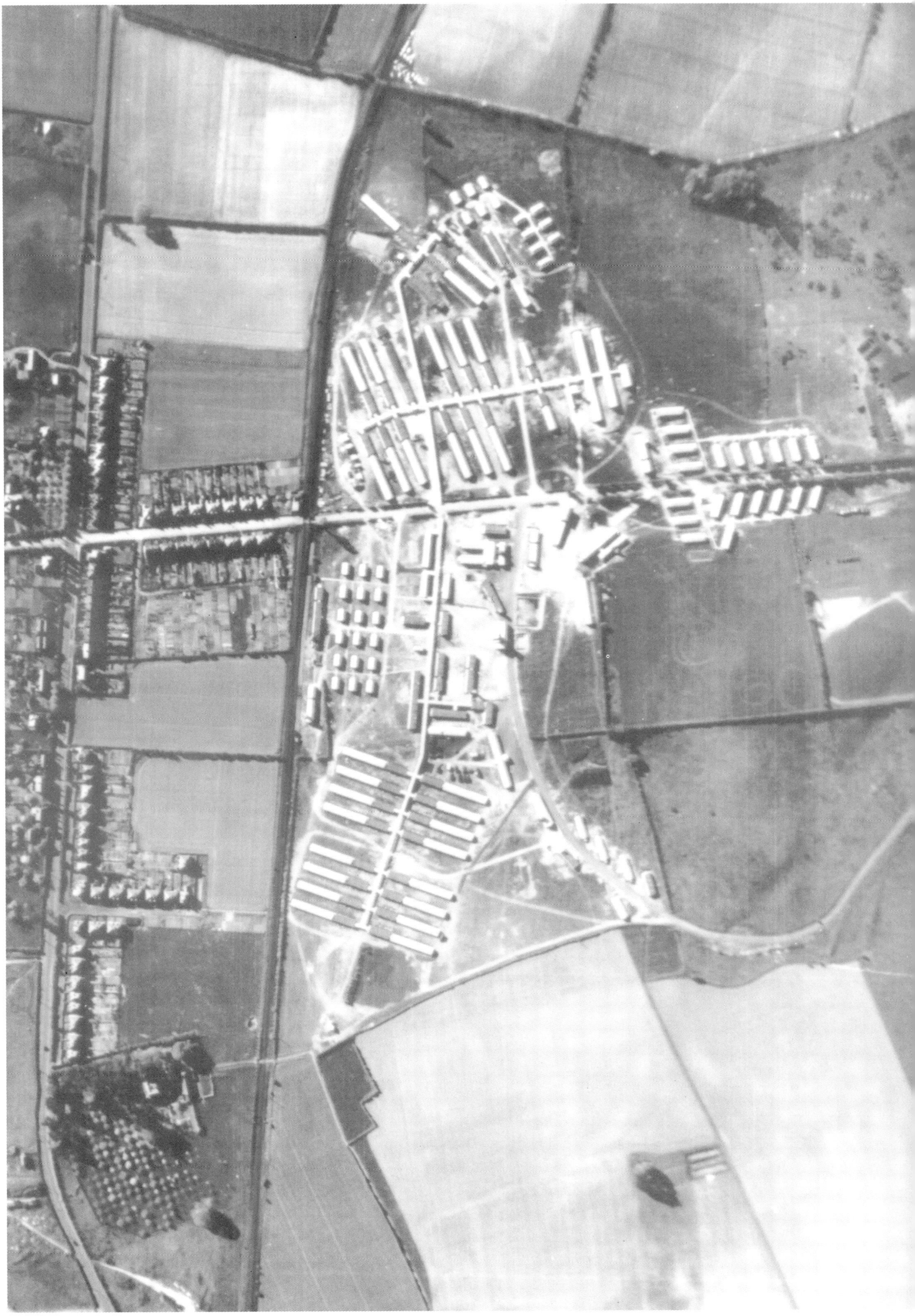

BEWDLEY CAMPS Nos. 1 & 2
4 MAY 1944
Photos taken by U.S.A.A.F
31st Photo Reconnaissance Squadron
10th Photographic Group
Aircraft : P38 Lightning
Based at Chalgrove, Oxfordshire
Photos courtesy : National Monuments Record
(English Heritage)

Stourport Regatta

The organisation was invited to participate in a boat regatta on the local Bank Holiday on the River Severn at Stourport. Two boats were entered and were rowed by Sgt John Morphy, Sgt Richard Cary, Sgt Lamont Johns, Lt Bentzen, Cpl Handler and Pfc John LaPolla. The hospital team returned triumphant in this event and were highly praised by members of the Regatta Committee.

297th Dance Orchestra

The orchestra was furnished with musical instruments procured through the Unit Fund. Other instruments and music was added by the Special Services Department when available.

The orchestra played for dances on the post held at the Officer's Club and for the Enlisted Men's dances. These dances were a semi-monthly affair and were looked forward to very much. Transportation was provided for young women from the surrounding area who attended the dances. Coffee, tea or cold drinks were served as well as sandwiches. The Recreation Building was open to all, and table tennis and snooker were enjoyed.

The band was successful in attracting large numbers of followers wherever they chanced to play. Many bookings were accepted and these included engagements in Wolverhampton, the University Overseas Club of Birmingham, the Gliderdrome in Kidderminster, the putting green in Stourport and for various organisations.

In April 1945 the band, consisting of 12 men, was sent to London on Detached Service for 5 days where they played at Rainbow Corner; after which a congratulatory letter followed, praising the work of the band and desiring them to play a return engagement.

The band also took part in a Dance Band Competition which was held in Malvern and they brought home second honors, losing only to the 825th Convalescent Center from Packington Hall, a group of seasoned veterans in the musical world.

War Orphan

The Detachment voluntarily raised £100 to sponsor a British War Orphan in the "Stars and Stripes" Orphan campaign in December 1944. The orphan, a little girl, visited the unit and was given a party in the enlisted men's mess hall during lunch where she was presented with a present from the Detachment and a special cake was baked for her. The band played during the meal and she was shown around the hospital area in the afternoon.

Chicago Tribune

During February 1945, through the auspices of the American Red Cross and the Public Relations Officer, United Kingdom Base, two reporters and a photographer from the Chicago Tribune spent a day at the hospital gathering material for a story concerning the unit, which was an affiliated unit from the Cook County Hospital, Chicago, Illinois.

Stanley Watkins of Bewdley remembers being taken with other pupils from Lax Lane School in U.S. Army trucks to visit the patients in the wards at the hospital. The children were thrilled with the amount of candies given to them by patients.

Enlisted Men's Barracks. 297 General Hospital.
Burlish Top in the background.

Enlisted Men's Barracks. 297 General Hospital.

Both photographs by Sergeant John P.Thomson (John Harper collection)

297th General Hospital Chapel

The Chapel was a "theater of operations" type chapel of British temporary construction. It had a small chancel on a slightly elevated platform with a built in pulpit on the left of the chancel. Folding chairs were provided for the chapel which had a seating capacity of 175. There were two offices, one for the Protestant Chaplain and one for the Roman Catholic Chaplain, and a washroom behind the chancel. A simple altar was built by one of the carpenters from the Utility Department and was stained and finished by one of the Chaplain's assistants. Red corduroy drapes, which had originally been purchased when the unit was in Temple, Texas, were hung behind the altar and some of the same material was used to complete the altar rail.

During the first few weeks, the Chaplain's assistants painted, varnished and waxed the concrete floor of the Chapel a dark red colour which gave the effect of a tile floor. A hemp matting was put down the centre aisle of the Chapel. All these decorations did much to create a worshipful atmosphere.

Two Roman Catholic masses were held each Sunday, one at 0800 hours and the other at 0930 hours. In addition to these Sunday masses a daily mass was held at 1755.

On 10 September 1944 a class of eight candidates for Confirmation were confirmed in the hospital Chapel by Roman Catholic Archbishop Williams of Birmingham.

Regular services were arranged on Friday evenings for Jewish personnel. Transportation was provided so that they could attend the New Year and Passover services at the Synagogue in Birmingham.

For Protestant personnel 52 Sunday worship services were held with a total attendance of 5,347, an average attendance of 103. On the first Sunday of each month the Sacrament of the Lord's Supper was observed and a total of 1,106 received communion. The largest attendance at any one service was on Easter Sunday 1945 morning at which 211 persons were present.

In an effort to provide religious life and inspiration to the patients in the hospital, regular visits were made by the chaplains to patients in the wards. When it was requested, Holy Communion was served to bed patients and bedside prayers were offered. A number of personal problems and opportunities to help the patients came to the attention of the chaplains during these ward calls. Testaments and other religious literature was given out as requested.

An important part of the work of the chaplains was the help which they were able to give the men in personal advice concerning a wide range of problems. These problems included worries over home conditions, difficulties in relationships with women, clashes with civil and military law, desires to obtain passes and furloughs, and other relationships which the soldier had with the army.

The Protestant Chaplain interviewed 27 couples wishing to get married and made reports to the Commanding Officer concerning the character and fitness of the fiancees for marriage.

RESTRICTED

HEADQUARTERS
297th (US) General Hospital
APO 640   US Army

7 August 1944

GENERAL ORDERS)
NUMBER .... 5)

OFF LIMITS

The following named establishments are declared OFF LIMITS to all members of this command:

RIVERSIDE CAFE
STOURPORT, WORCESTERSHIRE, ENGLAND

THE OLD ANCHOR INN
WORCESTER ROAD
STOURPORT, WORCESTERSHIRE, ENGLAND

By order of Colonel Pruitt:

HOWARD E. STINGEL
1st Lt., MAC
Adjutant.

RESTRICTED

HEADQUARTERS
297th (US) General Hospital
APO 121-A   US Army

8 October 1944

GENERAL ORDERS)
NUMBER .... 23)

OFF LIMITS

The following named establishment is declared OFF LIMITS to all members of this command:

JUBILEE DRIVE HOSTEL
Located about one half mile
south of KIDDERMINSTER, WORCESTERSHIRE,
ENGLAND

By order of Colonel Pruitt:

HOWARD E. STINGEL
1st Lt, MAC
Adjutant.

Reminiscences of a 297 GH Nurse

2nd Lt. Lillian R. Krell - N 757889 ANC.

Upon graduation in the October of 1943 I received my commission as a 2nd Lt. and reported to England General Hospital in Atlantic City, New Jersey for basic training on February 1st 1944. As I recall, I influenced my classmate, Matilda Glass, to join the Nurse Corps with me and together, we would "hup, two, three, four" on the boardwalk of Atlantic City.

Our first experience in dealing with "Army Protocol" occurred when we completed our four weeks of basic training and much to our disappointment, received separate nursing assignments. I was to report to Tilden General Hospital at Fort Dix, New Jersey, while my friend and classmate would be going on to Halloran General on Staten Island in New York. Of course, we reasoned, that this had to be a "gross mistake." After all, the Army had promised when we joined they would keep us together!

Since we knew "our rights" just having completed a course in "Army Grievance Procedures", we wrote a letter, signed jointly, to the Nurse Corps Adjutant of the First Service Command for a "hearing" relating to our complaints. Apparently our letter did make some waves. We received a response to report immediately to New York at the offices of the 1st Service Command for a personal hearing with the Adjutant. In no uncertain terms, we were informed that Army orders were "sealed in cement" and not to be questioned. Our orders would stand as issued, and in a curt command we were harshly ordered to leave our name, rank and serial number on her desk. We left that office "completely crushed" to go on to our respective new assignments as ordered!

As we were just beginning to adjust to our new post, the Adjutant must have had second thoughts about getting rid of the "two pains in the necks" because on April 1st, 1944 (my 22nd birthday) my friend and I received orders at our respective bases to join the 297th General Hospital going overseas!

It seemed no time at all after receiving our notification to join the 297 General Hospital that we found ourselves burdened with 40 lb field packs and struggling up the gangplank of the "Queen Elizabeth" on Memorial Day weekend of 1944.

I would not describe this trip as exactly a pleasure cruise. We were packed in like sardines - 10,000 battle ready troops and 75 nurses! Despite tight security in rerouting our troop transport train from New Jersey and boarding ship after midnight as a big 'security secret' we sailed from New York Harbor at high noon on Memorial Day 1944 with all New York standing on the dockside on this bright, clear sunny day to wave goodbye to our troop laden ship! (By now we were sure that all Germany knew that we were on the way).

Unfortunately, we hit stormy weather in mid-Atlantic with gale force winds increasing as we neared the Irish Sea. It seemed like a sheer miracle when we safely arrived in Gourock, Scotland, hours before dawn broke through the mist on 6th June 1944, D-Day. We waited on deck for hours in a cold light drizzle to be taken off the "Queen" by tender and put ashore. We were all deeply grateful to the British Red Cross Volunteers waiting for us in the wee hours of the morning with sandwiches and hot coffee.

We boarded a train soon after we disembarked for our destination in Llandudno, North Wales, where we would spend the next few days awaiting and assembling our

our medical supplies. It was at our Llandudno stop-off when we first learned of the D-Day invasion.

Again another long train ride across Wales and the cold, grey English countryside to Stourport on the Severn River, our final destination in the midlands of England.

The first order of the day at Camp Bewdley was to clean, sweep, scrub and whitewash walls until some sense of order made it possible to set up hospital beds and unpack medical supplies. I remember our nurses cutting up their cotton petticoats to provide much needed cleaning cloths.

The nurses' quarters were cold and damp. We literally had to stuff paper and whatever material we had on hand between the crevices of the wood to keep out the rain, wind and snow. Burlap Bags against the windows helped, but they could not, by any stretch of the imagination, be called attractive curtains! Our single pot belly stove in the middle of our hut, if overheated, tended to melt or disintegrate around the edges. Our standard joke was to cry out in desperation "Don't overheat the stove!"

The latrines were another problem in that we often had to walk through muddy, wet areas to get to them, and late at night it was difficult to find because of the enforced black-out regulations. Problems were even more magnified when fog enveloped the area! Something as simple as getting to the bathroom at night was for many of us a harrowing experience.

We barely had time to organize and set up our hospital when our first wounded patients arrived in convoy after convoy from the Normandy invasion combat area. In no time at all we were operating at full capacity and this did not let up until well after the Battle of the Bulge. Nurses worked 12-15 hour shifts and 24 hours around the clock whenever a new convoy of patients arrived. The 297th operated professionally as a team with great expertise. I felt truly fortunate to have been part of this dedicated team of physicians, nurses and corpsmen, as well as an administrative staff that functioned so effectively, providing our wounded men with the best possible medical/surgical services and supplies. Thanks to the new wonder drug called Penicillin, complications from wound infections were minimal.

Our American Red Cross provided much needed lifesaving plasma. New surgical techniques of bone grafting, developed by our fine orthopedic surgical team, saved many lives and limbs. I must give credit to the Army's amazing transportation system that was so effective in transporting patients from the battlefield to Army base hospitals in England so quickly. This above all, saved many lives.

The 297 General Hospital did not segregate its patients. However, our soldiers from the South went crazy when they saw local English girls eating and dancing, holding hands etc. with an African-American man. (In that era referred to as Negroes.) It caused many fist fights in the towns situated around the hospital. To ease the situation and simmer down the problem, all hospitals including the 297, 114 and 52 General issued separate passes for white and black military, that is alternate days for blacks and white. White and black soldiers on the base, amazingly enough, helped each other into wheelchairs and were nurturing and caring during their mutual recuperation.

As a young nurse I was assigned to several Rehabilitation Wards when the hospital opened as well as one or two Recovery Wards to supervise while on night duty. Since it was impossible to be everywhere at once I tended to divide my time between those wards that had more critical needs. The corpsmen on the Rehabilitation Wards were instructed to notify me if there were problems etc. Their main role was to provide nourishment, milk, juices etc, and tend to the basic comforts of these patients in a rehabilitation setting. I was very shocked to learn that we had VD cases in the Rehabilitation Wards that were under my supervision. Apparently our patients were getting out at night under the noses, so to speak, of our corpsmen. Since I was the officer in charge I had to take full responsibility. I was shocked! Talk about the teasing I had to take, particularly from our 'Smart Alec' male officers!

At this point I requested Col. Pruitt and my Chief Nurse to transfer me to the sickest Surgical Orthopedic floor where nearly every patient was in some kind of body cast. When Col. Pruitt asked why this particular type of Orthopedic Unit, my answer was swift and decisive ...."If any patient dares to move it is because I move them!"

After this event things changed quickly at the 297. Security increased at Camp Bewdley radically, especially at night! Nurses were no longer responsible for Rehbilitation Wards and corpsmen had to do bed checks several times during the night. Patients on report for rule infraction were warned that they would be 'shipped out' to active duty. It was going to be zero tolerance. The Medical Doctors would take turns planning health education programs and VD training films etc. This was to be ongoing for all rehabilitation and ambulatory patients. The places in town that appeared to be 'foci of infection' would be off limits. This would be enforced by the Military Police.

Major Hampar Kelikian who was in charge of the Orthopedic Surgical Wards and my Ward Officer was truly a shining star in our outfit. He saved many limbs through his early development of bone grafting procedures. Physicians from all over the E.T.O visited the 297th General Hospital to observe his operating technique. This man as a personality was so kind, gentle and loving, he never failed to come to our ward, no matter how late or tired he felt, to check out and chat with each patient. Major Kelikian was Armenian born and spoke with a heavy accent. It was typical of him to pull up a chair or sit at the edge of the bed and say," Sonny Boy. How are you feeling?" He called all his patients "Sonny Boy" and needless to say, these tough "Infantry Soldiers" would melt!

Major Kelikian, as a growing boy, had experienced great hunger and severe physical deprivation in his native Armenia during World War I. His country and its people were killed and displaced in that terrible "Holocaust" by the Ottoman Turks and the experience, mainly the fear of hunger never left him. For this reason he always carried a piece of bread and an onion with him when he left camp!

Special thanks to Mrs Lillian Swerdlow for permission to publish the above article and also to reproduce her wartime photographs.

SUMMER DAYS AT THE 297 GENERAL HOSPITAL

View of Nurses' Huts. Mount Pleasant in the background.
2nd. Lt. L.Krell in the foreground.

Photos : Lillian R.Swerdlow-Krell

Nurse Krell outside Hut 13, 'Last Chance'

2nd Lts Matilda Glass and Lillian Krell

Photo : Lillian R.Krell - Sherdlow

Interior of Nurses' Huts.   297 General Hospital .   April 1945

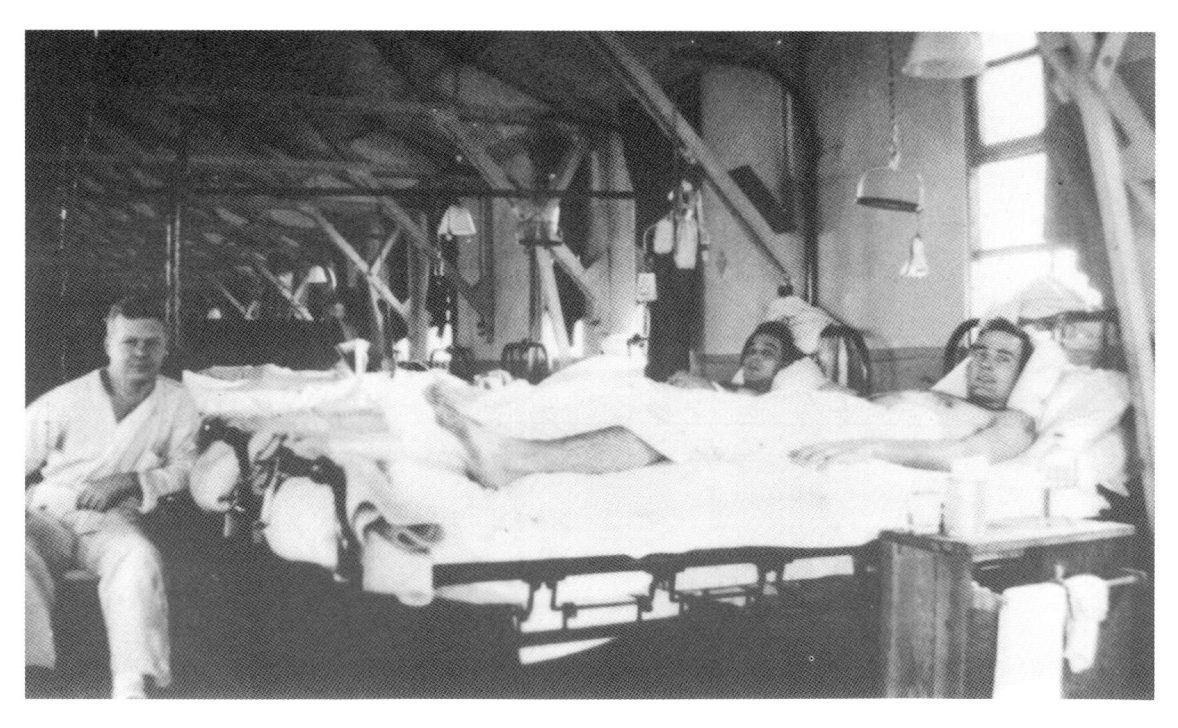

Photo : Lillian R.Krell-Sherdlow

Ward 15.   297 General Hospital.   March 1945

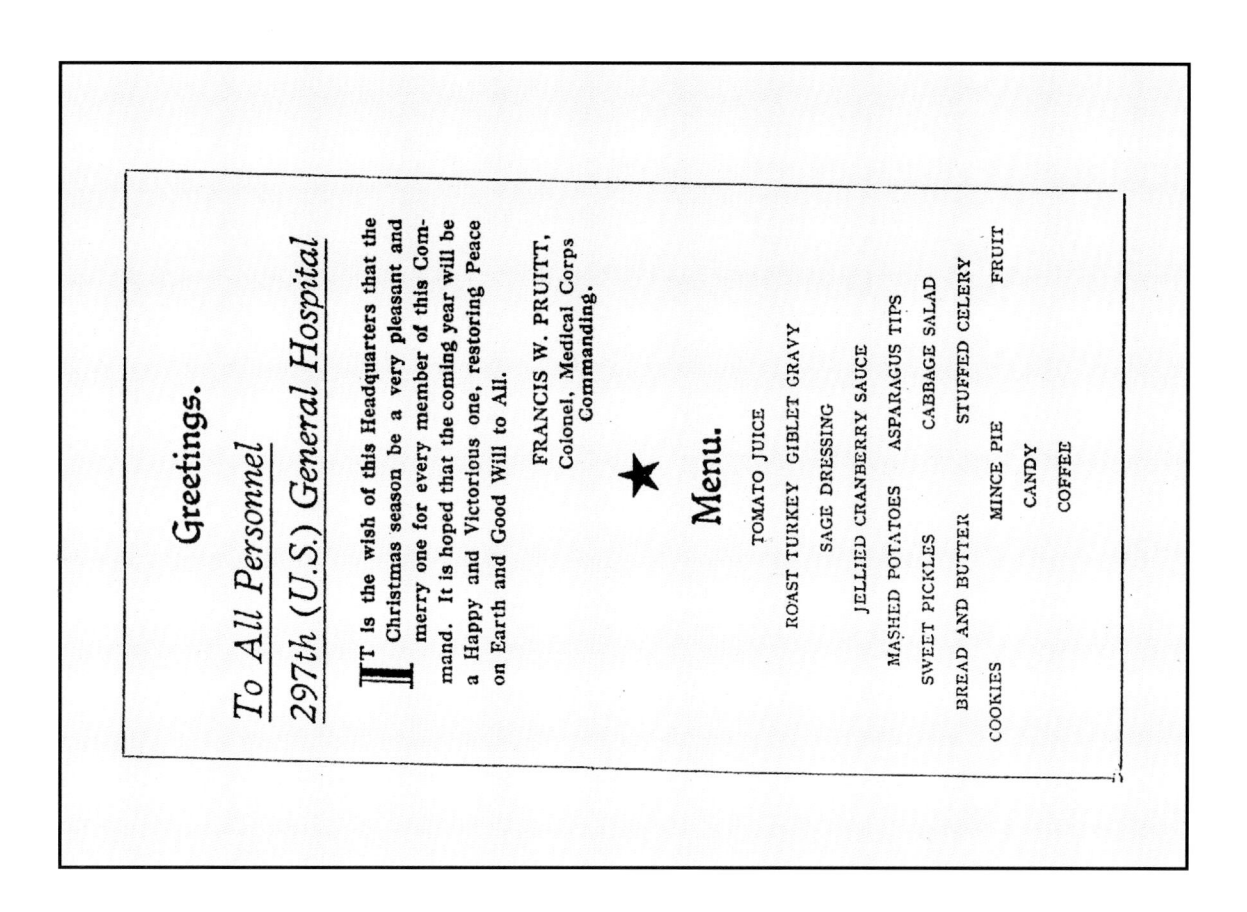

Greetings.

To All Personnel
297th (U.S.) General Hospital

It is the wish of this Headquarters that the Christmas season be a very pleasant and merry one for every member of this Command. It is hoped that the coming year will be a Happy and Victorious one, restoring Peace on Earth and Good Will to All.

FRANCIS W. PRUITT,
Colonel, Medical Corps
Commanding.

★

Menu.

TOMATO JUICE
ROAST TURKEY   GIBLET GRAVY
SAGE DRESSING
JELLIED CRANBERRY SAUCE
MASHED POTATOES   ASPARAGUS TIPS
SWEET PICKLES   CABBAGE SALAD
BREAD AND BUTTER   STUFFED CELERY
COOKIES   MINCE PIE   FRUIT
CANDY
COFFEE

Christmas, 1944

297th
General Hospital
ENGLAND

1944 Christmas Menu Card   297 General Hospital

Photo : Lillian R Swerdlow-Krell

The "Donutmobile" with patients at the 297 General Hospital

Nurses from the 297 General Hospital enjoying a day out.

Photo : Lillian R Swerdlow-Krell

Detachment Mess   297 General Hospital

Detachment Mess   297 General Hospital
Relaxing with bottles of Banks's beer!

Both photographs by Sergeant John P. Thomson (John Harper collection)

114th General Hospital

On 20 July 1944 the 114th General Hospital Unit departed from its home base at Fort Bragg, North Carolina, to a staging area for overseas movement at Camp Kilmer, New Jersey. Leaving the staging area on 25 July 1944 the unit travelled by rail to Harborside Terminal and thence by ferry to the pier in New York City to board a ship. The unit sailed, in a convoy, from New York on 26 July arriving at Gourock, Scotland, at 1530 on 5 August 1944.

The following day the unit was divided into two groups. The first group disembarked at 1000 and entrained at 1030 arriving at Bewdley station at 2000. The second group disembarked at 1100 and entrained at 1130 arriving at Bewdley station at 2400. The 297th General Hospital had made provisions to feed each group upon their arrival at Camp Bewdley.

On 7 August 1944 the unit began setting up hospital at Camp No.2 (Upper Camp) with the designation of U.S. Army Hospital Plant 4171.

The unit strength was as follows:

   58 Officers (55 assigned, 3 attached)
    1 Warrant Officer
   83 Nurses
    2 Hospital Dietitians
    2 Physical Therapy Aides
  452 Enlisted Men
    5 Red Cross Workers

One of the nurses, 2nd Lt Mary Ellen Nelson, on arriving at Bewdley in the middle of the night, must have been amazed to find that the unit's destination was within a mile or two of her birthplace in Peel Street in Kidderminster! Her family had emigrated to the U.S.A before the outbreak of war.

The hospital was opened at 0001 on 1 September 1944 for the reception of patients per par.1, General Order No.6, Headquarters, 114th General Hospital, with a bed capacity of 600 patients, with additional beds to be made available as required.

The first patient to be admitted was a member of the hospital staff. The first battle casualties to arrive at the hospital were transferred from the 156th General Hospital at Foxley, near Hereford, on 14 September 1944.

The first Hospital Train to arrive at the Stourport Railhead with patients for the 114th General Hospital arrived at 1715 on 20 September 1944. This was U.S.Army Hospital Train No.14, manned by the U.S 3rd Hospital Train Unit, based at Westbury, Wiltshire. The 292 patients were from U.S Army Plant 4121 (U.S Naval Base Hospital No.12, Navy 814 and 110th Station Hospital) at Netley, near Southampton. The majority of patients were battle casualties from France.

By November 1944 the bed capacity had been increased to 1,442 patients. The Neuropsychiatric Section was designated as a Combat Exhaustion Center. Seven wards were set aside for this center, three of which were double decked. Cases which could be rehabilitated were treated in accordance with the latest methods available.

The Rehabilitation Workshop was one of the outstanding features of this Neuropsychiatriac Section. At this shop patients were rehabilitated to regain their confidence in their ability to be useful and do useful duty. A variety of interesting forms of manual training were available: woodwork, metalwork, painting, sign painting, photography and their ability to be useful and do useful duty. A variety of interesting forms of manual training were available: woodwork, metalwork, painting, sign painting, photography and mechanical sections were available to suit the interest of the individual soldier. A G.M.C and an Austin motor were built from salvage parts collected and were useful in motor training. Many useful items were prepared by these patients for the use of patients on the wards, the various clinics and the messes of this hospital. To mention a few of these items, there were chart racks, metal waste paper baskets, bulletin boards, soiled linen containers, signs, ash trays and other items too numerous to mention.

The Stump Club

In December 1944, the current group of amputees, with the leadership of Lieutenant James Larso, organised what they called "The Stump Club". This organisation was comprised entirely of amputees and was complete with roster, officers, by-laws and even a mascot. This mascot was a product of the combined efforts of the club membership and was complete with pajamas, dog tags, amputation stump, traction apparatus and crutches. The value of this organisation was not only directed towards those who had formed it but also to the steadily increasing number of amputees who arrived at this hospital with each succeeding convoy.

The 114 General Hospital Historical Report comments as follows:

"It was really marvellous to see this group go into action upon the reception of a convoy. Each new amputee is beset by them hardly before the stretcher bearers have moved away from his bed, and even the most morose individual is no match for the Stump Club. It can be truthfully said that no amputee in this hospital has ever been given the opportunity to vegetate."

Ice Cream Parlor

A hut was obtained for use as a soda fountain and ice cream parlor. In this parlor a partition was erected, dividing the parlor into an enlisted men's section and an officer's section. Tables and booths were built in. The Coca-Cola machine was moved in from the Post Exchange and an electric ice cream freezer with 5 gallon freezing unit plus 80 gallons storage capacity was obtained and installed. Two civilian girls were hired to do the serving.

Prisoner of War Enclosure

During March 1944 a coloured unit, Company "C" of the 1329th G.S Regiment, comprising of 21 enlisted men were attached to the 297 General Hospital for rations and quarters to build a P.O.W enclosure on a site adjoining the 114 General Hospital.

200 German Prisoners of War arrived on 28 April 1945. A detachment of the 1362nd Military Labor Supervisory Company consisting of 2 Infantry Officers and 7 enlisted men were in charge of the enclosure, assisted by personnel of the 114 and 297 General Hospitals. These guards were quartered at the stockade.

The prisoners were used primarily in landscaping work, gardening, aiding in utilities and in cleaning the messes. A planned programme of painting of wards and buildings was carried out using P.O.W labour.

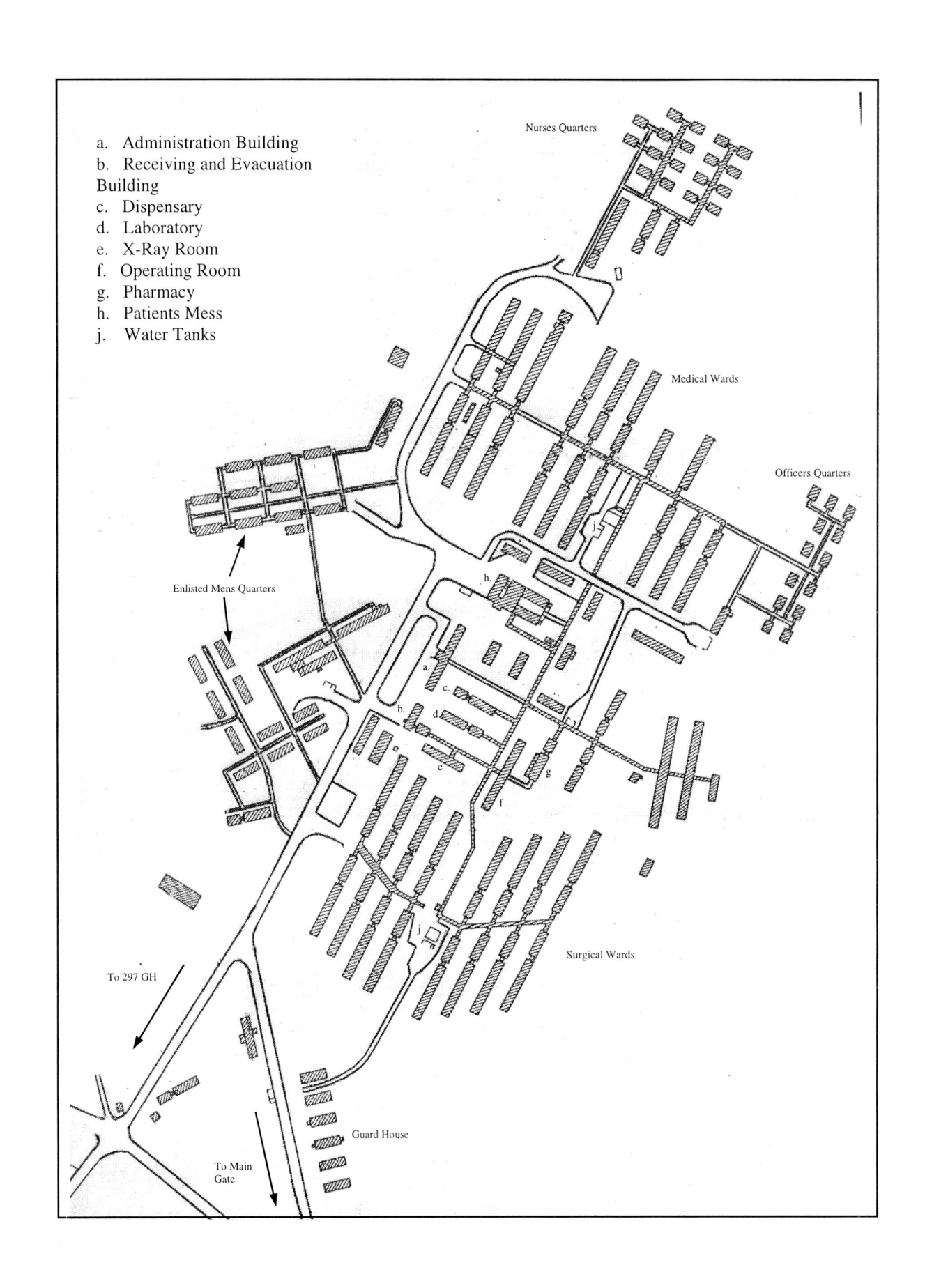

a. Administration Building
b. Receiving and Evacuation Building
c. Dispensary
d. Laboratory
e. X-Ray Room
f. Operating Room
g. Pharmacy
h. Patients Mess
j. Water Tanks

PLAN OF 114 GENERAL HOSPITAL

Organisation of 114 General Hospital   8 May 1945

ADMINISTRATIVE

Commanding Officer	Col. John B Chester
Executive Officer	Lt Col. Jose Maldonado
Adjutant	Capt Augustus Silva
Registrar	1st Lt Corbit T Provost
C.O Detachment of Patients	CWO Fletcher H Hall
Detachment Commander	Capt James E Marshall
Asst Detachment Commander	1st Lt David H Billyeald
Hospital Inspector	Major Anthony L Lombardi
General Supply Officer	Major William D Van Arnam
Medical Supply Officer	Capt Douglas R Chessher
Chief of Nursing Service	Capt Maree DeWitt
Mess Officer	1st Lt George W Jenkins
Dietitian	1st Lt Charlotte B Green
Transportation Officer	1st Lt Harry V Wilkinson Jr.
Protestant Chaplain	Capt Tommaso M Caliandro
Catholic Chaplain	1st Lt Senan D Kelly
Personnel Officer	1st Lt Anthony J DeLuca

PROFESSIONAL

Medical Service	Lt Col Mischa J Lustok
Asst. Chief Medical Service	Major Alfred Fleishman
Neuropsychiatric Section	Capt Mandel J Sachs
Asst. NP Section	Capt Robert J Van Amberg
Communicable Disease Section	Capt Richard W Payne
Gastro Intestinal Section	Capt Gunter M Elias
General Medicine Section	Capt James G Janney Jr.
Surgical Service	Lt Col Felix Jansey
Urological Section	Major William P Farber
Orthopedic Section	Major Donald B Sanford
E.E.N.T Section	Major Edwin S Wright
General Surgery Section	Major Vernon L Tuck
Anesthesia Section	Capt John E Kesterson
Rehabilitation Service	Major Clarence V Partridge
Laboratory Service	Lt Col William Rosenblatt
Dental Service	Lt Col Joe Minor
X-Ray Service	Major Luther M Vaughan
Physical Therapy	1st Lt Isabelle M Desmond

114th (US) GENERAL HOSPITAL
12th (US) HOSPITAL CENTER
OFFICE OF THE REGISTRAR
APO 121-A, U.S ARMY

21 May 1945

SUBJECT: Statistical Report for the period 1st January 1945 to 8 May 1945.

TO: The Commanding Officer, 114th (US) General Hospital, 12th Hospital Center, APO 121-A, U.S Army.

1. Remaining in Hospital as of 1st January 1945 1,371

2. Total Admissions for period: 2,048

    a. Surgical 997
    b. Medical 439
    c. Trench Foot 291
    d. Neuropsychiatric 297
    e. Quarters Cases 8
    f. Allied Personnel 11
    g. Carded for Record Only 5

3. Total Dispositions for Period: 3,099
    a. Zone of Interior:
        (1) Surgical 542
        (2) Medical 108
        (3) Trench Foot 189
        (4) Neuropsychiatric 238   1,077

    b. Duty:
        (1) Limited Assignment 1,030
        (2) General Assignment 486   1,516

    c. Transfers:
        (1) Convalescent Centers 324
        (2) Other Hospitals 156   480

    d. AWOL's 4

    e. Quarters 8

    f. Confinement 2

    g. Allied Personnel 11

    h. Death 1

4. Remaining in Hospital as of Midnight 8 May 1945 320

Total Patients for Period 3,419

Hospital Train Unloading Procedure

Upon notice of the pending arrival of a hospital train at the Stourport Railhead, a boarding party from the receiving hospital consisting of one Medical Officer and one Surgical Officer was assigned to board the train at a point about half an hours ride from the hospital detraining station. The Officers were accompanied by clerks from the Receiving and Evacuation Section who would tag the patients for the wards indicated by the Medical Officer.

In order to facilitate the ear-marking of patients to the proper ward and delivery of the patients so assigned, a sufficient number of tags (bearing the ward number) were prepared covering the number of beds available in each ward. Tags covering wards in the Surgical Section were coloured red, tags covering wards in the Medical Section were coloured blue and tags covering wards in the Officer's Section were coloured white.

For the unloading of hospital train cars, eight men teams were set up to detrain each car under the guidance of an NCO. Of these teams, four men would board the car and transfer the patient on a litter to the four men remaining on the ground who received the patient and loaded him on to the ambulance. Sufficient teams were trained in this manner so that all cars of a train could be detrained simultaneously.

Teams of five men, in charge of an NCO, were set up to detrain ambulatory patients, assisting them to dismount from the cars on a series of steps (Built by the Carpenter's Shop) and to guide them to buses or other vehicles used to transport them from the train to the hospital.

Within the hospital area, at dispersal points to which the patients were delivered by the ambulances, four man litter teams were stationed in sufficient numbers to handle the patients on litters from the ambulances to the wards. At these dispersal points, two man teams were also in attendance to redress the litters as soon as they were returned by the litter bearers from the wards and then load the dressed litter on to the ambulances returning to the train for additional patients.

Three dispersal areas were set up in the hospital grounds. The "Red Area" servicing the dispersal of patients assigned to the Surgical Section. The "Blue Area" servicing the dispersal of patients assigned to the Medical Section. The "White Area" serviced the Officers' Wards.

Although the majority of casualties arrived by hospital train a few were flown direct from the continent by C-47 aircraft to a nearby airfield, probably Halfpenny Green.

——— o-O-o ———

Departure from Camp Bewdley

On V-E Day, 8 May 1945, the 114 General Hospital had a census of 320 patients and the 297 General Hospital had 570 patients.

After V-E Day no convoys of patients in the direct line of evacuation were received by either hospital. However, a good number of admissions arrived as transfers from other hospitals that were being closed down.

Patients were evacuated from the hospitals in the normal way, the last patient leaving on 29 June 1945, the closing date of both hospitals.

In the period 30 June 1945 to 11 July 1945 all medical supplies were returned to depots and the site was prepared for turning over to the British authorities.

On 11 July 1945 the entire 114 and 297 hospital organisations moved with minimum essential equipment plus motor vehicles and all personnel to Hospital Plant 4169, Wolverley near Kidderminster, which had formerly been operated by the 52nd General Hospital, but was now designated to be used as a staging area for the 114 and 297 General Hospitals.

The living quarters at Wolverley were far superior to those at Camp Bewdley. To the nurses the Quonset living quarters seemed palatial after the crowded, cold, primitive huts that they had previously. The Quonset facilities were roomy, warm and most of all they enjoyed the hot showers and bathroom facilities in each unit. There was also a well designed theater where they could view up to date films on a large screen. Also without patient care responsibilities they were able to go sightseeing around neighbouring towns.

On 24 and 25 August 1945 the personnel finally departed from Kidderminster by train for Southampton where they boarded the liner "Queen Elizabeth". At 1330 hours on 26 August 1945 the "Queen Elizabeth" set sail arriving at New York at 1230 hours on 31 August 1945.

The New York Daily News for 1 September 1945 reported the arrival in New York:

QUEEN ELIZABETH STEAMS IN AND 14,860 ABOARD GO NUTS.

"With music by Cab Calloway and Sammy Kaye and their bands, with 14,860 fighting men throwing neckties, shirts and even shoes into the air, with Colonel Jimmy Stewart and ex-Governer Herbert Lehman aboard, the Queen Elizabeth, the mightiest troop transport of them all, slid up against Pier 90 at the foot of 50th Street in the Hudson yesterday at noon.

It was an arrival to put all previous arrivals in the shade as the GIs went nuts and the hotstuff bands gave their collective impression of how to carve a rug to shreds when the boys come home. The racket split the steaming air over the Hudson and bounced off the Jersey cliffs. The whole show made Ladies' Day at Ebbets Field seem like Sunday afternoon in Trinity churchyard.

Col Stewart, the movie man turned hero for real, was back with his Croix de Guerre and Palm, his Distinguished Flying Cross and his Air Medal and Oak Leaf Cluster.

Lehman was back from his job as director of the United Nations Relief and Rehabilitation Administration. His wife was with him. Aboard also were Dr. Stephen S Wise, president of the World Jewish Congress and Mrs Wise. They had been in London attending the World Zionist Conference.

And on the bridge, a smile on his face and more than a hint of mist in his eyes as he watched the joyous scene on the deck below stood the ranking officer aboard, Brig. Gen William M Goss, commander of the 2nd Combat Wing of the 8th Air Force, Col Jimmy's outfit.

The great steamer had a varied passenger list. In addition to 8th Air Force units, the Queen brought home three General Hospital units with more than 270 nurses, five companies of Negro soldiers, 900 Navy personnel, 2,000 infantry replacements and about 1,000 men who had been stationed in Iceland"

Photo : National Archives

The "Queen Elizabeth", her decks loaded with returning troops,
in New York Harbor, 1945

---

55 years after the departure of the U.S Army from Camp Bewdley there is very little evidence remaining of the two large installations which had a very important role in the Second World War.

The main gate posts can still be seen on the winding road leading from the Kidderminster to Stourport main road to the nature reserve on Burlish Top. In the nature reserve itself the concrete roadways and paths of the upper camp can still be traced.

The lower camp has been replaced by a housing estate, although a few concrete bases of the enlisted men's huts can still be seen amongst the undergrowth on the right hand side of the road leading from Burlish Crossing to the nature reserve at Burlish Top. A brick water tower, which probably served the lower camp, can be seen on the Mount Pleasant hillside.

Photo : Aerofilms Ltd

Dog Lane Camp, Bewdley
Photographed 1952

Dog Lane Camp, Bewdley

There was a small hutted camp here which was used by the U.S Army during 1944. A XII Corps station list dated 7 June 1944 gives the 576th Ordnance Ammunition Company as being stationed at Bewdley. This was probably one of the units at Dog Lane.

Lax Lane Depot, Bewdley

U.S Army Quartermaster Truck Companies operated from this depot. The trucks were kept in the adjacent Gardners Meadow.

Amongst their duties was taking empty Jerrycans to the petrol store at Chadwick Bank, Stourport for filling. The cans were subsequently despatched by rail to the south of England.

Welcome Club, Bewdley

During February 1944 a Welcome Club was opened in Bewdley at the WVS Headquarters above the 'Chocolate Box' in Load Street. (the premises now occupied by the HSBC Bank). The main function of the Welcome Clubs was to bring the GIs into amicable contact with the local civilians.

52nd General Hospital
Hospital Plant 4169   Wolverley

The 52nd General Hospital Unit left Camp Kilmer, New Jersey, on 5 January 1943 and boarded the "Queen Elizabeth" as part of Task Force 2266 for the crossing to the European Theater of Operations, arriving in Glasgow in pouring rain on 11 January 1943. The next stage of the journey involved a long train ride, in crowded conditions, to Taunton which was to be the staging area for the unit.

While at Norton Manor, Taunton, the transportation personnel made a trip to the U.S Army Depot at Ashchurch to pick up the unit's transportation consisting of 21 assorted vehicles. The return trip was a nightmare with vehicles breaking down every few miles, drivers unfamiliar with English road courtesy and the blackout. To make matters worse the Quartermaster leading the string of vehicles turned into a blind alley in the centre of Bristol which almost disrupted the lines of communication within the city itself in the attempt to get all out and under way again. Despite this, all personnel and vehicles arrived tired but safely back at camp.

The Adjutant, 2nd Lt. John F.Marsellus, effected plans for the transfer of the entire personnel from Norton Manor, Taunton to Camp Wolverley, Kidderminster. In addition to the troop movement it was necessary to arrange for the reception of the organisation at its destination : Rations, Quarters, heating facilities, transportation from the railway station to the camp, transportation records and the immediate opening of the Headquarters. An advance detachment of officers and men were despatched to Wolverley to proceed with the cleaning up of the installation and making it habitable for the main body.

The move to Wolverley was made on 17 February 1943, the trip was uneventful, no breakdowns, and a distance of approximately 130 miles was covered in about 8 1/2 hours, roughly averaging 15 miles per hour for the 24 vehicles and 3 trailers. Meanwhile the main body of men travelled by train to Kidderminster railway station where transport was waiting to convey them to Wolverley.

The Medical Inspector reported that the entire camp was in a poor condition from the sanitary viewpoint, despite considerable effort in preliminary cleaning of roads and floors which had been effected by the advance party. There was no surface drainage whatsoever, it was true the camp was on a hillside, but pools of water tended to accumulate in relatively low spots on pavements and soil. Debris incidental to construction work was strewn throughout the area and there were two enormous dump heaps.

There were 25 or 30 freight cars loaded with medical supplies at Kidderminster Goods Depot, several days overdue for unloading, with demurage charges accumulating.

The hospital was officially opened to patients on 15 April 1943. At this time there were only 7 Medical Wards and 2 Surgical Wards in active function, the rest were serviced and held in readiness. During the period of gradual increasing clinical work, structural and supply defects were corrected, the floors were resurfaced and the grounds were landscaped.

The formal opening of the Red Cross recreation building was celebrated by inviting the enlisted men to an open house evening occasion and by having a tea party for patients, officers, nurses and key people in the community. About 200 guests came during the afternoon of the latter occasion, among them the Mayor of Kidderminster, his wife and daughter, members of the British Red Cross, Women's Voluntary Service, Y.M.C.A, Women's Institute, Rotarians, local teachers and librarians.

The Red Cross Clubmobile called at the post once a week. About 1500 doughnuts and 25 gallons of coffee were served on each visit.

Colonel Neville H.McNerney assumed command on 1 May 1943 and the entire hospital personnel were immediately inspired by his leadership and able direction.

On 3 August 1943 the entire personnel of the 52nd General Hospital were shocked by the sudden death of the Catholic Chaplain, Father William A.Irwin. Father Irwin had been with the unit from the beginning and though he had been hospitalised for a time following a heart attack and his ultimate return to the States was imminent, he was back at his post and feeling quite fit when this second and fatal attack occurred. A full military funeral was extended to Father Irwin on the afternoon of the day he died, with a High Mass chanted by Father Wilfred Gladu, his newly assigned successor. Following the Mass a brief and moving eulogy was delivered by Father Callahan of the 10th Replacement Depot. Immediately following the Catholic Service a General Memorial Service was conducted by the Protestant Chaplain, Lt. Truesdell, who eulogised Father Irwin warmly and impressively. Later that day Father Irwin's remains were shipped to London for interment at Brookwood National Cemetery.

On 4 September 1943, to commemorate the first anniversary of the activation of the unit, Brigadier General Paul R.L.Hawley, the Chief Surgeon, European Theater of Operations, visited the post. After a formal inspection of the Detachment, the Chief Surgeon was escorted by the Commanding Officer, Colonel McNerney, for an official tour of the entire hospital. All Services, Sections and Departments were covered and passed. General Hawley presented to Sergeant Elmer L.Burger, one of the patients, the Distinguished Flying Cross and two Clusters, Air Medal and three clusters and the Purple Heart. The latter was awarded on 8 July 1943 by Colonel McNerney for wounds received in a crash landing in the Sfax area.

On 4 September 1943, 97 patients were admitted to the Medical Wards from North Africa. They remained for 18 days as boarders, not calling for active medical care. These patients were ambulatory having been previously disposed of for shipment back to the United States.

On 24 September 1943, 153 patients were admitted for reclassification from Iceland, most of these were maladjusted neuropsychiatric patients, about 40% being boarded to the Zone of the Interior, the rest being sent to non tactical outfits.

On 28 October 1943, the 52nd General Hospital received the distinction of being the first American hospital in the European Theater of Operations to receive repatriated prisoners of war from Germany. An exchange of Allied and German prisoners of war had been arranged through the neutral Swedish Government, this exchange took place at Gothenburg where Hospital Ship No.33'"Atlantis" took on 790 repatriated Allied servicemen including 17 American servicemen. The "Atlantis" arrived in Liverpool alongside the Princes Landing Stage on Tuesday 26 October 1943. The American servicemen sent to Wolverley included two officers and nine enlisted men who had either landed from the air on enemy territory or had been captured on the field of battle. As most of these patients were members of the United States Army Air Force, Brigadier General Malcolm Grow, the Chief Surgeon of the Eighth Air Force, made a personal visit to the hospital to welcome them back to the care of the American authorities. In recognition of wounds received in action Colonel McNerny, the Commanding Officer, awarded and presented the repatriates with the Purple Heart.

Under the direction of the Special Service Department a campaign was instituted to solicit funds for the "Stars and Stripes" War Orphan Fund. A total contribution of £436-8-0 was collected from the personnel of this command. The hospital was commended by the American Red Cross and the administrators of the fund, for this remarkable contribution was one of the largest single donations by any organisation in the theater. The amount was sufficient to sponsor four war orphans for a period of five years each. A party was held for the four orphans adapted by the organisation, a cake was made for each. The enlisted mens mess was attractively decorated for the occasion.

Fourteen USO shows were presented on the post during 1943 for the benefit of both patients and all personnel of the command. They were met with an enthusiastic response from all attending. The most popular presentation proved to be the Bob Hope show. Several British musical companies presented revues at the Post Theater which gave a personal glimpse of the famed acts of the British music halls.

One of the highlights of the Supply branch of the Quartermaster Service was the organisation and running of the ration breakdown point which for the latter part of 1943 had been feeding on average 3,000 personnel daily. This included receipt and issue of all food for same and also the running of a cold storage warehouse at nearby Stourport.

The hospital wound up the first 8 1/2 months of operation with a total of 3,774 patients admitted, of these 24 were classed as battle casualties.

During the Christmas holidays many parties were sponsored by both the officers and the local Red Cross in the interest of the enlisted men. The officers staged a party for the enlisted men in their recreation hall on Christmas Eve and gifts were distributed to the enlisted men. Beer and refreshments were served during the course of the evening.

During December the hospital was honoured by the official visits of ranking American and British dignitaries. These included the presence of Major General John C.H Lee, Commanding General, Services of Supply, ETOUSA at Christmas dinner followed by an inspection of the Post.

On New Years Day the enlisted men sponsored a party for 250 children of Kidderminster and Wolverley. Judging by the enthusiasm displayed by the children the party proved to be very successful. They were escorted to the theater, shown a moving picture and presented with packages of candy and chewing gum. The Mayor of Kidderminster said a few words of appreciation.

During February 1944 facilities were established on the post for the transmittal of the American Forces Network, an all G.I daily radio program originating in London and carried by wire to this station. The transmitter had a range of approximately 30 miles and the network was picked up by other American installations within that radius. The Special Service Section installed radios in all wards and occupied ward tents. The A.F.N personnel stationed on the post were on duty from 0730 until 2300 at the relay station to give the area the finest reception possible. Needless to say the radio programs were greatly appreciated, particularly by the patients.

During April and May 1944 the hospital was functioning more or less as a large Station Hospital caring for a division (90th Infantry) and a great many small units.

During this period the entire command became conscious of "big things to come". An expansion program was embarked upon whereby the ward accommodation facilities were increased by 40% by the erection of ward tents adjacent to the existing ward

The program of erecting these tents with cement foundations, completely furnished with beds, stoves, cabinets etc. was accomplished by the unit enlisted personnel, without the aid of outside agencies, after duty hours at a time when the detachment was under strength because of various groups being on detached service at other locations.

D-Day, 6 June 1944 was not in itself the culminating date of these preparations insofar as the hospital was concerned. The climax was reached five days later at 1030 hours with the arrival of the first hospital train transporting casualties from the initial phases of the invasion of France. Using eight ambulances and seven trucks it took two hours and fiftyfive minutes to unload the 252 litter and 64 ambulatory patients. It was found that the two miles from the railway station to the hospital required about 35 to 40 minutes before a vehicle could get back to the station to get more patients. The 12th Hospital Center loaned ambulances for the trains that came after and the fourth train was unloaded in about an hour and a half.

Four trains were received in June as follows:

Date	Source	Litter Patients	Ambulatory Patients
11 June 1944	110 Station Hospital (Netley)	252	64
13 June 1944	38 Station Hospital (Winchester)	119	107
15 June 1944	315 Station Hospital (Axminster)	134	143
22 June 1944	347 Station Hospital (Marlborough)	170	136

On 16 June 1944, recognising the need for prompt consideration of justifiable claims for the Purple Heart Award, the Commanding Officer established a board of three officers to certify the eligibility of individuals to receive this award for wounds received in the face of enemy action. The machinery was immediately installed providing medical officers with certificate forms indicating proper procedure, and the certification to the necessity of medical treatment, recommendation of the board and action by the Commanding Officer. Up to 30 June 1944 the hospital had processed and awarded 822 Purple Hearts and 14 Oak Leaf Clusters, all to casualties of the operations in establishing a beachhead on the coast of France.

One of the functions which the Medical Supply Department had plenty of experience of at this time was the exchange of linen from hospital trains. Each time a train arrived with patients a truck was loaded with clean sheets, pillow cases, pajamas, robes, towels etc. and delivered to the train in exchange for a like amount of soiled linen.

The American Red Cross workers at the hospital had their first experience of meeting the mass needs of the very recent casualties admitted in large numbers from hospital trains. A system was worked out whereby each one of these new patients were seen on an individual basis within eight hours of admission. He was given all his comfort supply needs and helped to write that first letter to best meet his family's questions within censorship regulations. If he was unable to do this he had the proven assurance of help within the next 24 hours.

Since casualties began arriving from France the American Red Cross workers at the hospital were deluged with offers of volunteer help from the community. Sixteen additional volunteers, plus three each day loaned by Miss Jameson from her Red Cross Club, formed a group of six to ten women daily to help with bandage rolling and surgical supplies. Miss Villiger, director of another Red Cross Club, had her volunteers making 200 bedside ditty bags each month from extra G.I towels that the Quartermaster was able to obtain. Miss Jameson, from the Donut Dugout in Kidderminster, provided at a moments notice doughnuts for a most welcome midnight snack for patients who arrived in the middle of the night.

Joe Louis, the World Heavyweight Boxing Champion, with his entourage visited the hospital on 16 June 1944 accompanied by Lt. Havilland and 1st. Sgt George Nicholson, Louis's sparring partner. They made a whirlwind tour of all the wards where they were met with popular acclaim. The bed patients were visibly impressed as evidenced by their free conversation with the Champ. Many patients and hospital personnel had a photographic record of his visit.

During July four trains were received with another 1,124 patients, the process for receiving these trains was improved as a result of experience bringing the unloading time down to about an hour. On 25 July 1944 there were 1,536 patients in the hospital which was the highest number to date.

The total number of civilian personnel employed at the hospital at the end of September was 32, ten of these worked in the mess halls and the others mostly worked for the Utilities Section as plumbers, electricians, stokers etc.

U.S.O Camp shows were presented,one of which was highlighted by the personal appearance of Warner Brothers Hollywood star Miss Irene Manning. Miss Bebe Daniels, popular star of stage, screen and radio also visited the hospital on several occasions. Recordings were made while Miss Daniels interviewed the patients and the discs were shipped back to the United States to be transcribed on the Purple Heart Hour over the NBC Network.

The 1944 Christmas holiday season was featured by a party given by the enlisted men for the benefit of children of British servicemen. They toured the grounds, visited patients on the wards, were given ice cream and coke in the patient's mess and were shown a movie at the theater. Each child was provided with a gift of cookies, gum and candies before they departed on the bus for their homes. Approximately 300 children attended the party.

By 31 December 1944 twenty hospital trains had been received since D-Day bringing nearly 6,000 battle casualties. The total number of patients that had been admitted up to this date since the hospital opened was 16,643.

The hospital was full during January and February 1945 partly because there was an influx of patients from what has now become known as the "Battle of the Bulge". In March and April there was a decline in admissions until at one point there were fewer than 300 patients in the plant.

V-E Day, 8 May 1945 was met with a solemn thanksgiving rather than riotous hilarity. To all, it meant that for the first time in three years they could take a deep sigh of relief with visions of universal peace in sight.

The 25 May 1945 marked the appearance of German POWs on the post. Their taking over of many labour and fatigue details dealing with maintenance and policing were of material assistance.

On 29 June 1945 the 52nd General Hospital was officially closed for the reception of patients as of 2400 hours.

Photo : National Archives

Buildings and grounds of 52nd. General Hospital, Wolverley

Photo : National Archives

Main road with Receiving and Evacuating building at extreme right with main administration building next to it.

48th Field Hospital

APO 403　　　　　　　　Telephone No. Kidderminster 3251

On 29 March 1944 the 48th Field Hospital Unit, consisting of 18 nurses, 190 enlisted men and 22 officers, departed from Fort Jackson S.C for Camp Kilmer, New Jersey. Final preparations for movement overseas were completed at Camp Kilmer and the unit left New York Port of Embarkation on 6 April 1944. Debarkation was accomplished on 16 April 1944 at Glasgow, Scotland. On 17 April 1944 all personnel arrived at Kidderminster, Worcestershire, England. Immediately upon arrival in England the unit was transferred from the Army Service Force to the Third United States Army.

On 7 June 1944, 12 officers, 14 nurses and 22 enlisted men from the 4th Auxiliary Surgical Group were attached to this unit. Two female American Red Cross workers also joined the unit on 17 June 1944.

Three months at Kidderminster were spent in obtaining, working with, and preparing equipment for overseas shipment and combat use. During this stay in England the newly issued equipment was modified to better suit the anticipated needs of a field hospital. Each platoon set up its hospital numerous times in darkness and inclement weather. All platoons separately spent at least 5 consecutive days in the field setting up hospital. Plans were formulated for three different methods of setting up a field hospital.

For recreation the men availed themselves of facilities such as public swimming and public dancing in Kidderminster. In addition to this, beer parties and dances for the men were held when possible.

After arrival in England, the Army Nurse Corps were at first busy procuring equipment and maintaining physical condition. The training program included gymnasium activities almost daily for two hours, marches every other day graduated from 4 miles to 12 miles and overnight bivouac every week. On 15 May supplies were obtained, and the nurses began preparing some of them for hospital use. June was spent in making supplies and improvising, organizing and packing hospital equipment. Training in setting up a hospital was thorough.

All personnel departed from Kidderminster, England on 10 July 1944 and arrived at Seton Barracks, Plymouth on the same date. Final preparations for movement to the continent were made while at Seton Barracks.

Before leaving Kidderminster attempts had been made to have the hospital equipment accompany the personnel. A final decision to leave the equipment under guard at Kidderminster (where it was to be loaded and sent to the continent by a medical depot) was handed down after a telephone conversation with transportation corps officers at European Theater of Operations, U.S Army Headquarters in London. The equipment was then left behind with a guard from a nearby hospital unit, despite the desire of the commanding officer of this unit to leave unit rear guards behind.

After arrival on the continent, the Surgeon of the Third U.S Army was informed that the equipment was left at Kidderminster and many efforts were made to get it shipped. The equipment finally arrived at Cherbourg, France on 7 August 1944. Although two enlisted men and an officer checked the equipment as it was unloaded, over 400 boxes were lost. A search of all dumps was made and some missing boxes were found. On 31 December 1944 about 85% of the missing equipment had been replaced.

47th Field Hospital

APO 403 Telephone No. Kidderminster 3128

Unit strength : 22 Officers
  18 Nurses
  190 Enlisted men

This unit arrived in England with the 48th Field Hospital as part of shipment 5221.

On departure from Kidderminster the 47th Field Hospital landed on Omah Beach on 22 June 1944.

While at Kidderminster the 47th Field Hospital was probably at the Greatfield Hall camp (Birchfield Road) and the 48th Field at the Rifle Range camp.

Finance Disbursing Units

On 7 November 1943 the 52nd Finance Disbursing Section was established at Camp Wolverley as the central disbursing office for U.S Army installations in the surrounding vicinity. This facilitated and accelerated the transaction of fiscal activities by the presence of trained staff to advise on fiscal matters and the elimination of the necessity to travel to distant parts.

The 52nd Finance Disbursing Unit was replaced at Camp Wolverley on 15 June 1944 by the 88th Finance Disbursng Unit.

Army Postal Units

A main post office was established at Camp Wolverley to expedite the forwarding and receiving of all official and personal mail. The 651st Army Postal Unit was assigned to run this office on 31 March 1943.

On 24 June 1944 the 651st Army Postal Unit was replaced by Detachment A of the 121st Army Postal Unit serving the 52nd, 114th and 297th General Hospitals.

Donut Dugout – Kidderminster

In March 1944 the American Red Cross opened a club in Arch Hill, Kidderminster for the benefit of American servicemen. The club was called the 'Donut Dugout'. Miss Martyn Jameson from California was in charge, and with the assistance of local civilians, midnight snacks of doughnuts and coffee were available as well as clean, neat surroundings for lounging and writing.

------ o O o ------

Official Souvenir Programme

KIDDERMINSTER'S "Salute the Soldier" CAMPAIGN.

6th TO 13th MAY 1944 — £300,000 COST OF MOVING 3 DIVISIONS TO BERLIN — 6th TO 13th MAY 1944

PRICE THREEPENCE

At 12.30 on Saturday 6 May Major General G. Cook, Commanding General XII Corps, U.S Army, accompanied by his Chief of Staff, Colonel Ralph J.Canine, and his two aides, Captain Garret J. Garretson II and 1st. Lt. John B.Kling attended a luncheon given by the Mayor of Kidderminster, Alderman L.Tolley, at the Lion Hotel, Kidderminster. This event officially began the 'Salute the Soldier' week.

"Salute the Soldier"

A GRAND ANGLO-AMERICAN Popular BALL

The GLIDERDROME BALLROOM

Thursday, May 11th
8 p.m. UNTIL MIDNIGHT.

The FAMOUS AMERICAN ARMY DANCE BAND
of the 24 Special Service Corps (14 members) directed by SGT. DAVID (by kind permission of Commanding Officer).

THE R.A.P.C.A.T.S. DANCE ORCHESTRA and Broadcasting Swingtette with "Buddy"
(by kind permission of Officer Commanding).

Fully Licensed BAR. BUFFET

ADMISSION—
Civilians and Officers 3/6;
Forces (Non-Com. Ranks) 2/6

A GRAND SELECT GALA BALL

M.C.: Mr. ERNEST RICHARDS.

The TOWN HALL

Saturday, May 13th

Patrons: The Mayor and Mayoress (Alderman and Mrs. L. Tolley).

With **KIDDERMINSTER'S OWN BROADCASTING BANDS**

THE R.A.P.C.A.T.S.
(by kind permission of Col. Hollingsworth),
and
FRED REYNOLDS' DANCE ORCHESTRA

Non-Stop Dancing—8 p.m. until Midnight Special Decorations. Buffet. Fully Licensed Bar. Valuable Prizes. Old and Modern Dancing

ADMISSION—
Civilians and Officers 5/- ;
Forces (Non-Com. Ranks) 3/6

Get your tickets now and avoid disappointment !
Obtainable from all Savings Group Secretaries.

Ceremonial Parade of all Services, assembling on Brinton Park at 3 p.m. :

GREATEST MILITARY SPECTACLE EVER STAGED IN KIDDERMINSTER.

Mobile Section will leave at 3-35 p.m.
Marching Section at 3-40 p.m. prompt, along the following route :— Talbot Street, Sutton Road, Bewdley Street, Park Butts, Bull Ring, Vicar Street, **Saluting Base**, Oxford Street, Bridge Street, New Road, Stourport Road, to Brinton Park to dismiss.

Dismissal Speech to the Services will be made by His Worship the Mayor (Alderman Tolley). National Anthems will be played by the Band of the Worcestershire Regiment.

SHOW YOUR ENTHUSIASM BY DISPLAYING FLAGS.

In order to ensure the success of the Ceremonial Rally of the various Services and Demonstration at the Park, will the Public kindly co-operate by keeping off the Parade Ground and also control Children.

Officer Commanding Parade :—Major A. F. R. Godfrey, General List Infantry.
Parade Marshals : Messrs. J. H. Whicheloe, W. A Davies, R. A. Longmore, A. S. Rogers, F. A. Kettle.

KIDDERMINSTER "SALUTE THE SOLDIER" WEEK

Photo : Courtesy Worcester Evening News

The U.S Army 90th Infantry Division Band passing the saluting base in Vicar Street, Kidderminster, on Saturday 6th May 1944.

TO THOSE WHO ARE GIVING ALL.

SALUTING BASE :—ROWLAND HILL STATUE.

The Salute will be taken by Col. K. J. Martin, D.S.O., A.D.C. supported on the Platform by His Worship the Mayor of Kidderminster (Alderman L. Tolley), the Mayoress (Mrs. L. Tolley), High Constable, H. C. Carter, Esq., Lord Winster and Geoffrey S. Tomkinson, Esq., O.B.E., M.C., J.P. (Chairman Kidderminster Savings Committee). Also supporting :— Col. Hollingsworth, R.A.P.C., Col. R. W. A. Painter, M.C. (Commanding " O " Sector Worc. Sub. District) and other distinguished serving Officers with Members of the Town Council and Savings Officials.

Dipping of Standards to serving soldiers by a detachment of British Legion.

The Kidderminster Prize Band will play a Selection of Music from 3 p.m. to 3-50 p.m.

A Running Commentary of the Parade will be broadcast from the Town Hall by Major Robinson, of 22nd Battn. Staffs. Home Guard.

There will be a Public Address prior to the March Past.
Speaker : Col. K. J. Martin, D.S.O., A.D.C.,
supported by His Worship the Mayor (Alderman L. Tolley).

Salute the Soldier with Your Pocket. Speed up the Target like a Rocket.

90th Infantry Division

357th Infantry Regiment

The 357th Infantry Regiment moved to the New York port of embarkation on the 22 March 1944. They boarded the "Dominion Monarch", a 27,000 ton British ex luxury liner which had been converted into a troop transport and turned over to the United States Army by the British Government. The 13 day voyage was without particular interest from a seaman's point of view, but many of the land-lubbers spent considerable time feeding the fish, and expected to be sent to the bottom any day by U-boats.

The "Dominion Monarch" docked at Mersey Docks, Liverpool, England, on the 4th April 1944. After debarking at 1630, the troops loaded immediately on trains and moved to Kinlet Park, near Bewdley. All elements of the Regiment were quartered here except the 1st Battalion which was quartered at Camp Gatacre nearby.

Intensive training was begun immediately with stress being placed on speed marches with heavy loads of weapons and ammunition. Covering 5 miles on foot in less than an hour was the way it went. This can and will be appreciated only by those readers who have walked up the steep English hills and who realize that the average rate of march for foot troops is only 2 1/2 miles per hour.

During the stay at Kinlet Park, the men were granted short passes to nearby towns. These soldiers , however, were not here for fun, but for the most serious business they had ever undertaken - and they knew it. Besides, when evening came, a few hours rest was what was wanted most.

On the 13th May the Regiment moved 64 miles nearer to the English Channel to Chepstow.

358th Infantry Regiment

On 22 March 1944 troops of the 358th Infantry Regiment rode the rails to New York Harbor, where under the cover of darkness they boarded the M.S "John Erickson". On the second night out to sea the liner was forced to put back into port for engine repairs, but after three days she again put out to sea and proceeded across the Atlantic without further incident. So it was a welcome sight indeed on Easter Sunday, the eighth of April, when troops of the Regiment looked out on Liverpool Harbor.

At Liverpool the Regiment was hustled aboard English trains and transported across the neatly patterned countryside to two camps just south of Birmingham. The Second and Third Battalions, and the Special Units were billeted at Camp Sturt Common near the town of Bewdley, while the First Battalion was at Camp Coton Hall. Training began immediately with special emphasis on physical conditioning exercises and marches over the picturesque English countryside. Daily the men were required to carry full combat equipment on fast road marches. Another hike was added to the busy schedule for some when they set out for the nearby villages of Kidderminster and Bewdley, where local atmosphere as well as ale was absorbed.

On 12th May the units moved to Llanmartin, near Newport, South Wales before landing on Utah beach on the 8th June 1944.

90th Infantry Division
Location of elements of Division at 31 May 1944

		Unit strength
90th Division Headquarters	Birmingham	158
HQ Company	Birmingham	107
Military Police Platoon	Birmingham	73
Band	Birmingham	58
357th Infantry Regiment Headquarters	Kinlet	
2nd and 3rd Battalions	Kinlet	
1st Battalion	Gatacre Hall	3,118
358th Infantry Regiment Headquarters	Sturt Common	
2nd and 3rd Battalions	Sturt Common	
1st Battalion	Coton Hall	3,118
359th Infantry Regiment Headquarters	Leominster	
2nd and 3rd Battalions	Leominster	
1st Battalion	Willey Moor	3,118
90th Division Artillery Headquarters	Davenport House	114
343rd Field Artillery Battalion	Davenport House	509
344th Field Artillery Battalion	Davenport House	509
345th Field Artillery Battalion	Davenport House	527
915th Field Artillery Battalion	Davenport House	509
90th Quartermaster Company	Coton Hall	193
90th Signal Company	Birmingham	226
90th Recce Troop	Willey Moor	155
315th Engineer Battalion Headquarters	Leominster	
A Company	Davenport House	
B Company	Kinlet	
C Company	Willey Moor	647
315th Medical Battalion Headquarters	Birmingham	
A Company	Chepstow	
B Company	Chepstow	
C Company	Leominster	
D Company	Kinlet	465
790th Ordnance Company	Arundel Castle	193

LOCATION OF U.S ARMY CAMPS
31 MAY 1944

- STANLEY HALL
- DAVENPORT HOUSE
- CHYKNELL HOUSE
- *Bridgnorth   + Halfpenny Green Airfield
- GATACRE HOUSE

- COTON HALL   • ENVILLE

- KINLET PARK

  WOLVERLEY
  52nd GENERAL HOSPITAL

- STURT COMMON   BLAKEDOWN DEPOT DP2-G24

- MAWLEY HALL   • BEWDLEY   • KIDDERMINSTER

- CAMP BEWDLEY. XII CORPS HQ.

  *Stourport

• U.S. Army Camp

AJT 12/99

Source : MRU. ETOUSA Station List dated 31 May 1944.

Tented U.S Army Camps in district

<u>Sturt Common</u>
  Units staging included :
Headquarters and 2 Battalions of 358th Infantry Regiment

<u>Kinlet Park</u>
  Units staging included :
    Headquarters and 2 Battallions of 357th Infantry Regiment
    3rd Cavalry Group
    43rd Cavalry Squadron
    B Company, 315th Engineer Battalion
    D Company, 315th Medical Battalion
    253rd Armd. Field Artillery Battalion

<u>Coton Hall</u>
  Units staging included
    Battallion of 358th Infantry Regiment
    90th Quartermaster Company
    93rd Signal Battallion

<u>Gatacre Hall</u>
  Units staging included :
    Battalion of 357th Infantry Regiment
    240th Field Artillery Battalion (155 mm gun)

<u>Davenport House</u>
  Units staging included :
    90th Division Artillery Headquarters
    343rd Field Artillery Battalion (105 mm howitzer)
    344th Field Artillery Battalion (105 mm howitzer)
    345th Field Artillery Battalion (155 mm howitzer)
    915th Field Artillery Battalion (105 mm howitzer)
    274th Armd. Field Artillery Battalion

<u>Chyknell House</u>
  Units staging included :
    445th Q.M Troop Transport Company
    642nd Q.M Troop Transport Company
    3918th Q.M Gas Supply Company
    3919th Q.M Gas Supply Company
    3920th Q.M Gas Supply Company

<u>Enville</u>
  Units staging included :
    687th Field Artillery Battalion (105mm howitzer)

Stanley Hall, Bridgnorth
Units staging included :
447th Q.M Troop Transport Company
448th Q.M Troop Transport Company
3200th Q.M Service Company
3201st Q.M Service Company

Mawley Hall, Cleobury
Unit staging :
221st Signal Depot Company

Catherton Common
Unit staging :
463rd Anti-aircraft Artillery Battalion

- - - - - - 0 0 0 - - - - - -

Supply Depot DP2 - G24   Blakedown

On 29 January 1944 a detachment of the 554 Q.M Railhead Company arrived at Camp Bewdley to set up and operate a ration distribution point for the combat troops stationed in the district.

The distribution point was set up at Blakedown, adjacent to Churchill and Blakedown railway station. The installation was a sub depot to the giant General Stores Depot G24 at Honeybourne.

On 10 June 1944, one officer and 69 enlisted men were relieved from attachment to DP2-G24 and left Blakedown at 0752 hours by train en route for Plymouth, where they boarded the "Empress Anvil" on 14 June arriving in France the following day.

They were replaced at Blakedown by another Railhead Company, the depot continuing to supply the hospitals at Camp Bewdley and Wolverley in addition to the combat troops in the Wyre Forest area.

The depot ceased to function during the summer of 1945 upon the closure of the hospitals.

Hospital Trains

The war years brought many interesting locomotive types and train workings through Kidderminster, but probably those which created the most excitement among the schoolboy railway enthusiasts on the 'Wooden Bridge' were the U.S Army Overseas Ambulance Trains.(Designated Hospital Trains by the U.S Army).

These trains were intended for use on the continent after the Allied landings in France and were converted from stock of the four main line companies. Each train of 14 or 15 coaches consisted of Ward Cars, Pharmacy Car complete with operating theatre, Kitchen/Dining Car, Personnel Sleeping Cars and Stores Cars.

Ten of these trains, plus a spare, were allocated for U.S Army use in Britain for a period from D-Day, 6th June 1944, onwards. As they were Westinghouse brake fitted and had to be capable of traversing branch lines such as the Kington branch, L.N.E.R class B12/3 locomotives were selected as suitable motive power. In addition to the 46 medical staff resident on the train, 7 L.N.E.R train crew, consisting of 2 drivers, 2 firemen, 2 guards and a fitter were also quartered and subsisted on the train. The patient capacity of each train varied between 292 and 316.

Casualties were brought across the English Channel in hospital ships and other available naval craft and unloaded at Southampton and other suitable landing points in Dorset and Devon. Other casualties were airlifted to various airfields in the south of England. They were then taken by road ambulance to nearby transit hospitals, where they were processed and given medical treatment before being transported by hospital train to general hospitals situated in central England and Wales.

An L.N.E.R class B12/3 4-6-0 locomotive was permanently attached to each train, in steam, so that it could be called into service at a moment's notice. At D-Day the 10 trains were stabled as follows:

    4 at U.S Army Depot G47 at Westbury, Wilts
    2 at U.S Army Depot G45 at Newbury Racecourse
    2 at Bournemouth West carriage sidings
    1 at Exeter (GWR)
    1 at Templecombe

The first arrival at Kidderminster of a U.S Army Hospital Train with casualties from the initial phases of the invasion of France was at 10.30 on the morning of 11th June 1944. L.N.E,R B12/3 No. 8518, piloted by G.W.R mogul No.7308, with 14 L.N.E.R coaches, painted in a dull green livery with red crosses on the sides and roofs, came from the Worcester direction and proceeded through the down goods loop to a siding adjacent to the goods shed.

The first U.S Army Hospital Train arrived at Stourport on the evening of 19th July 1944 hauled by L.N.E.R B12/3 No.8516.

The Overseas type Hospital Trains (OAT) continued to arrive at Kidderminster and Stourport until the end of November 1944 when they had all been prepared for shipment to France. Arrivals after then were the Home Ambulance Trains (HAT) which usually consisted of 12 coaches manned by about 24 medical staff. Also occasionally used were Casualty Evacuation Trains (CET), which were not favoured by the Americans. They were very basic and were originally used for moving civilian patients from hospitals in areas subject to bombing.

HOSPITAL TRAINS OPERATED BY U.S ARMY

Train No.	Type	Litter Patients	Ambulatory Patients	Total Patients	Stabling Points	H.Train Unit
11	OAT	228	64	292	Exeter Westbury	4th
12	OAT	228	64	292	Newbury G45	23rd
13	OAT	228	64	292	Newbury G45	7th
14	OAT	228	64	292	Westbury G47	3rd
15	OAT	252	64	316	Westbury G47	44th
17	OAT	240	64	304	Westbury G47	45th
27	OAT	252	64	316	Bournemouth West	43rd
31	OAT	252	64	316	Bournemouth West	21st
33	OAT	231	64	295	Westbury G47	24th
36	OAT	231	64	295	Templecombe	1st
37	OAT	231	64	295	Newbury G45 Westbury GWR	7th 8th
1	HAT	168	112	280	Westbury GWR	12th
2	HAT	192	128	320	Westbury GWR Southampton	12th
55	HAT	126	158	284	Taunton Dover Sudbury (Staffs)	8th
57	HAT	126	158	284	Malvern Wells	5th
59	HAT	126	158	284	Swindon	6th
61	HAT	126	158	284	Sudbury (Staffs)	5th
64	HAT	126	158	284	Newbury G45	6th
67	HAT	198	64	262	Bournemouth West Dover	59th
68	HAT	198	64	262	Bournemouth West Dover	58th
69	HAT	198	64	262	Bournemouth West Southampton Malvern Wells	58th
70	HAT	198	64	262	Westbury GWR	57th
71	HAT	216	64	280	Westbury GWR	57th
72	HAT	216	64	280	Bournemouth West Taunton	59th
316	CET	324	-	324	Westbury GWR Bournemouth West Southampton	8th

OAT = Overseas Ambulance Train   HAT = Home Ambulance Train
CET = Casualty Evacuation Train

HOSPITAL TRAINS TO STOURPORT FOR 114 AND 297 GENERAL HOSPITALS

Date	Train No.	No. of Patients	Entraining Station
19-7-44	11	292	Axminster
23-7-44	14	292	Swindon
28-7-44	12	292	
2-8-44	17	304	
15-8-44	14	292	Netley
20-9-44	14	292	Netley
22-9-44		292	
5-10-44		292	
16-10-44		296	
24-10-44	14	292	Chiseldon
26-10-44		292	Southampton
7-11-44		292	
17-11-44		293	
26-11-44		240	
29-11-44	2	313	Southampton, Stockbridge
3-12-44		288	
7-12-44			
10-12-44			
19-12-44	2	318	Stockbridge
29-12-44	2	318	Southampton
31-12-44	2	320	Chiseldon
6-1-45			
8-1-45			
13-1-45		270	
25-1-45			
5-2-45			
17-2-45	67	247	Southampton
27-2-45	316	322	
-3-45			
9-3-45			
-3-45			
-4-45			
20-4-45		301	
3-5-45		307	
-5-45		268	

Photo : National Archives

Patients being unloaded from U.S Army operated British built Hospital Train No. 15 at Saint Quentin, France. Train No. 15 came to Kidderminster on 22 June 1944 with patients for the 52nd General Hospital at Wolverley.

Photo : H.C. Casserley

L.N.E.R Class B12/3 No. 8516. This locomotive brought the first Hospital Train to Stourport with patients for the 297 General Hospital on 19 July 1944.

SOUTHERN RAILWAY

SPECIAL NOTICE AMB. No. 1, 1944.

AMBULANCE TRAINS

This Notice supersedes Special Notice Amb. No. 1, 1940.

OPERATION OF AUSTERITY (U.S.A.) AMBULANCE TRAINS.
LIST OF ENTRAINING AND DETRAINING STATIONS AND ROUTES, &c.

To	Route	Schedule No.	To	Route	Schedule No.
From Tavistock.					
Taunton	} Exeter St. Davids	53	Kidderminster	} Exeter St. Davids	53
Bristol T.M.			Overton-on-Dee (A)		
Cirencester (W'moor)			Sudbury (Staffs.)		
Malvern Wells L.M.S.					
From Axminster.					
Taunton	Exeter	56	Bristol T.M.	Yeovil	50
Cirencester	Andover Jc.	48	Malvern Wells	Templecombe	51
Kidderminster	Salisbury	44	Overton-on-Dee (A)	Salisbury	44
Sudbury (Staffs.)	Templecombe	51			
From Sherborne.					
Taunton	Exeter St. Davids	55	Bristol T.M.	Yeovil	54
Cirencester	Andover Jc.	49	Malvern Wells	Templecombe	52
Kidderminster	Salisbury	46	Overton-on-Dee (A)	Salisbury	46
Sudbury (Staffs.)	Templecombe	52			
From Wimborne.					
Taunton	Broadstone, Templecombe and Exeter.	58	Bristol T.M.	Salisbury	2
Cirencester	Andover Jc.	1	Malvern Wells	Broadstone and Bath	60
Kidderminster	Salisbury	2	Overton-on-Dee (A)	Salisbury	2
Sudbury (Staffs.)	Broadstone and S.&D.	60			
From Netley.					
Taunton	Salisbury	26	Bristol T.M.	Salisbury	26
Cirencester	Andover Jc.	25	Malvern Wells	Salisbury	26
Kidderminster	Salisbury	26	Overton-on-Dee (A)	Salisbury	26
Sudbury (Staffs.)	Salisbury	26			
From Stockbridge.					
Taunton	Salisbury	28	Bristol T.M.	Salisbury	28
Cirencester	Andover Jc.	27	Malvern Wells	Salisbury	28
Kidderminster	Salisbury	28	Overton-on-Dee (A)	Salisbury	28
Sudbury (Staffs.)	Salisbury	28			

A—Home Ambulance trains only.

— 6 —

OPERATION OF AUSTERITY (U.S.A.) AMBULANCE TRAINS.
LIST OF ENTRAINING AND DETRAINING STATIONS AND ROUTES, &c.—*continued.*

To	Route	Schedule No.	To	Route	Schedule No.
From Bailey Gate.					
Taunton	Templecombe and Exeter.	58	—	—	—
From Ringwood.					
Taunton	Broadstone, Templecombe and Exeter.	57	Bristol T.M.	Salisbury	5
			Malvern Wells	Broadstone and Bath	59
Cirencester	Andover Jc.	4	Overton-on-Dee (A)	Salisbury	5
Kidderminster	Salisbury	5			
Sudbury (Staffs.)	Broadstone and S.&D.	59			
From Wool.					
Taunton	Dorchester	92	Bristol T.M.	Salisbury	90
Cirencester	Andover Jc.	89	Malvern Wells	Broadstone and S.&D.	91
Kidderminster	Salisbury	90	Overton-on-Dee	Salisbury	90
Sudbury (Staffs)	Broadstone and S.&D.	91			

A—Home Ambulance trains only.

Extracts from Southern Railway Special Notice AMB 1, 1944 concerning ambulance trains, Kidderminster being listed as a detraining station. The GWR would have issued a similar notice listing entraining stations on their territory, such as Swindon, Chiseldon, Marlborough and Newbury.